HUMAN PSYCHOLOGY

LEARNERS MINDSET

DR. MUKTA GOYAL

Made with ♥ on the Notion Press Platform
www.notionpress.com

Contents

Preface   *v*

Acknowledgements   *vii*

1. CREATIVITY & WORKPLACE   1

2. FREUD'S PSYCHOANALYTIC THEORY ON PERSONALITY: 9
   FEMINIST APPROACHES ON GENDER CONSTRUCTION

3. UNDERSTANDING AND MANAGING DISRUPTIVE BEHAVIOR   25
   IN ADOLESCENTS

4. A LANGUAGE DEVELOPMENT AT EARLY AGE AND ITS   37
   THEORIES

5. COGNITIVE AND MORAL DEVELOPMENT IN LEARNERS   48

6. PERSONALITY CONCEPTS AND THEORIES   59

7. UNDERSTANDING THE DEVELOPMENTAL CHARACTERISTICS   69
   OF THE LEARNER

8. ADJUSTMENT CONCEPT PROCESS OF ADJUSTMENT AND   79
   DEFENCE MECHANISM

9. THE INVENTION OF CREATIVITY: THE EMERGENCE OF A   85
   DISCOURSE

10. THE CONCEPT OF INTELLIGENCE: USEFUL OR USELESS?   100

11. LANGUAGE DEVELOPMENT IN LEARNERS   110

12. INTELLIGENCE AND CREATIVITY   118

13. PSYCHOLOGY OF LEARNERS AND BETTERMENT OF   130
    LEARNER'S ATTITUDES IN LEARNING PROCESS

14. LEARNING THEORIES OF PERSONALITY: IVAN PAVLOV   139

List of Authors   147

Preface

Psychologists often define learning as a relatively permanent change in behaviour as a result of experience. The psychology of learning focuses on a range of topics related to how people learn and interact with their environments. Psychology, the behaviourists believed, should be the scientific study of observable behaviour. Behaviourism thrived during the first half of the twentieth century and contributed a great deal to our understanding of some important learning processes.

Our mind-sets also affect whether we seek out and persist through challenges, whether we think others should be given opportunities to learn, whether we get depressed, even whether we act prejudiced. In short, mind-sets are important. Imparting a new mind-set successfully requires a careful application of persuasion principles.

This book help students to organize their thinking about psychology at a conceptual level. Psychological science has much to contribute to enhancing teaching and learning in the classroom. Teaching and learning are intricately linked to social and behavioural factors of human development, including cognition, motivation, social interaction, and communication. This book is designed to facilitate these learning outcomes, Psychology in Everyday Life: Each chapter contains one or two features designed to link the principles from the chapter to real-world applications in business, environment, health, law, learning, and other relevant domains.

Dr.Mukta Gupta

ACKNOWLEDGEMENTS

Primarily I would like to thank God for being able to complete this book with success. Then I would like to thanks my family, and authors of this book, without their contribution this book would not have been a complete pool of knowledge.

I would also like heartfelt thanks to my friends for their extensible support.

Dr.Mukta Gupta

I

CREATIVITY & WORKPLACE

Dr.Anshika Rajvanshi, *Assistant Professor, Department of Management, IIMT, Delhi,*

ABSTRACT:

"Creativity is seeing what everyone else has seen and thinking what no one else has thought." -Albert Einstein

The author believes that creativity is a collection of traits rather than a single trait. Intelligence, intense interest, knowledge, originality (ideas), creative instinct, nonconformity, courage, and persistence are basic elements of the concept of creativity. Creativity can manifest itself in a variety of areas of life, and at various stages, some of them are more prominent than others. The author tried to contribute the importance of Creativity at workplace which can result in significant works that benefit society as a whole and bring fame for the organization.

INTRODUCTION:

When we hear a word Creative we start thinking about different people who are involved in various creative tasks such as artist, painter, photographer, an author, may be a film maker or a chef or we start thinking of people who make things and we label them as creative type. But in reality there is no such word as creative type and every one of us is creative in some or the other aspects. Creativity can't be defined in one way but can be expressed differently. Creativity involves making things but it also involve mashing up ideas in different ways, it can mean thinking differently about data and finding unique solutions to varied practical problems, it can mean hacking system and tuning in different way, it can be exploring ideas and navigating information, it can mean designing system that empowers the creative work of others, it can mean creating change to the world and may be interaction with people etc. These approaches shape our work in a profound ways. The morale says that by looking at the creative side we should look out the creativity in ourselves.

The act of making new and imaginative ideas a reality is referred to as creativity. Creativity is defined as the ability to perceive the world in novel ways, to uncover hidden patterns, to connect seemingly unrelated phenomena, and to generate solutions. Creativity is comprised of two processes: thinking and producing.

A person is imaginative but not creative if he has ideas but do not act on them. Creativity is a combinatorial force: it is our ability to tap into our "inner" pool of resources – knowledge, insight, information, inspiration, and all the fragments populating our minds that we have accumulated over the years simply by being present, alive, and awake to the world, and to combine them in extraordinary new ways.

Components of Creativity:

There are two components for showing your creativity. One should have the courage to carry out it on a regular basis.

Originality: This aspect talks about that what so ever you have in your brain should be unique and not simply an extension of something else which already exist in the environment.

Functionality: This is related to that the idea must actually work or be useful in some way for the purpose it has generated.

Types of Creativity

Various Experts talked about various types of creativity. According to the "four c" model of creativity, there are four types:

"Mini-c" creativity entails personally meaningful ideas and insights known only to the self.

"Little-c" creativity is mostly concerned with everyday thinking and problem-solving. This type of creativity assists people in solving everyday problems and adapting to changing environments.

"Pro-C" Professionals who are skilled and creative in their respective fields engage in "Pro-C" creativity. These people are creative in their vocation or profession, but they do not achieve eminence for their work.

"Big-C" creativity entails producing works and ideas that are regarded as outstanding in their respective fields. This type of creativity leads to eminence and acclaim, and it frequently results in world-changing creations such as medical breakthroughs, technological advancements, and artistic accomplishments.

What it takes to be Creative: According to Csikszentmihalyi, creative people have a number of characteristics that contribute to their innovative thinking. Among these important characteristics are:

Energy: Creative people have an abundance of both physical and mental energy. They do, however, spend a lot of time quietly thinking and reflecting.

Intelligence: For many years, psychologists have believed that intelligence plays an important role in creativity. Researchers discovered in Terman's famous longitudinal study of gifted children that, while high IQ is required for great creativity, not all people with high IQs are creative. Csikszentmihalyi believes that creative people must be smart, but they must also be capable of seeing things in new ways, even if they are familiar.

Discipline: Creative people do not sit around waiting for inspiration. They are playful while also being disciplined in their pursuit of their work and passions.

While some people appear to be born with a natural gift for creativity, there are things you can do to improve your own. According to Csikszentmihalyi, creativity necessitates both a fresh perspective and discipline.

Creativity at workplace

Employees are more likely to collaborate when they are inspired to be creative. When they have new ideas, they seek feedback from colleagues. The creative process, by definition, encourages collaboration, and this is the most important advantage of providing a workplace conducive to creative thinking.

Now the question arises when does creativity happen at workplace? The answer of the question lies in itself and dependent on the willingness and positive attitude of a person to find out the solutions for the different problems.

Mihaly Csikszentmihalyi, a psychologist, suggested in his book Creativity: Flow and the Psychology of Discovery and Invention that creativity can be seen in a variety of situations.

- When People are stimulating, interesting, and to have a wide range of unusual thoughts.
- When People see the world through new eyes, have insightful ideas, and make significant personal discoveries.
- When people achieve great creative accomplishments that are known throughout the world. The best example of this may include inventor Thomas Edison and artists Pablo Picasso.

When coming up with a solution to a problem, people with creative minds usually follow a process. This procedure frequently includes the following steps:

1. **Planning and conducting research:** This step involves gathering materials and conducting specific research on the task or problem at hand. You also conduct more general research on the subject and may employ more external information when problem-solving.

2. **Problem-solving meditation:** Instead of attempting to find a clear solution to the problem, begin to think deeply about it and experiment with various ideas that may eventually lead to a solution.

3. **Disconnection from the issue:** In this step, you take a long break from working on or thinking about the problem and potential solutions.

4. **Allowing your idea to return to you:** After fully removing yourself from the problem for a specified period of time, you will frequently gain new insight.

5. **Developing and implementing the concept:** Finally, you will be able to expand on your concept and apply it to your work. During this stage, you may want to consider sharing your idea with others to get feedback so that you can improve it further.

Benefits of Creative Workplace

Now day's companies are giving liberty to their employees to take part in Brainstorming sessions. They are also boost about being Innovative and creative but we are still way back in many of the aspects as creativity should be the continuous task in an organization. There may be few benefits which an organization may achieve by fostering creativity.

Better Team work and Team Building: Employees are more likely to collaborate when they are inspired to be creative. When they have new ideas, they seek feedback from colleagues. The creative process, by definition, encourages collaboration, and this is the most important advantage of providing a workplace conducive to creative thinking. Team bonding also contributes to employee engagement. Interactions are more likely among coworkers, even if they do not work together on a regular basis. A higher level of comfort in a team is beneficial to any organisation.

Improved Employee Attraction and Retention: Companies can attract more talented professionals by creating an environment that encourages creative thinking. They can fill positions in a more effective and efficient manner. Current employees experience a similar effect, as they are more likely to stay on board as a result of the creative environment. They become satisfied with their work and commit to it.

Problem-solving Abilities: The most important aspect of creativity, without a doubt, is how it affects the work. Employees who can think creatively and outside the box are more likely to come up with unique and innovative solutions to problems they face. This eagerness to solve problems can lead to novel approaches to completing tasks and running the organisation more efficiently.

Fostering creativity at work place

Creating the right working environment is critical for increasing employee productivity. This is based on scientific evidence. According to the study 'Happiness Works,' millennials expect to be happy at work and see their jobs as more of a valuable life experience than a paycheck.

Encourage both individualism and alliance: The strange thing about collaboration is that it necessitates both individuality and selflessness. Managers must not only encourage team bonding and collaborative work, but also ensure that employees' individuality is not checked at the door. Many unique ideas originate with a single person but are shaped by a team to become fully formed.

Never, Ever Say No: The brainstorming process can be delicate and complicated, particularly when a large team is working closely to find a strong solution. In these circumstances, it is all too easy to pass judgement on an idea and dismiss it as unsuitable. Rather than allowing negativity to stifle growth, promote positive and additive feedback. The phrase "yes and..." can go a long way toward assisting the entire team and they may associated with the organization for a long term.

Make Your Team More Diverse: To accelerate problem-solving, one simple and quick way to create a more creative workplace is to include a variety of perspectives, insights, and learning styles. The so-called Medici effect, proposed by author Frans Johansson, contends that diverse teams are more likely to generate innovative ideas due to the various approaches to a problem.

Encourage creativity in the workplace through Office Design: An inspiring work environment fosters creativity and innovation. Even if your office layout consists primarily of cubicles rather than open space, there are still ways to make employees feel inspired by their surroundings. You can, for example, encourage employees to bring in photos, prints, or small decorative items from home.

Allow for freedom and flexibility in how work is completed: Creativity in the workplace does not have to mean workplace creativity. A change of scenery can sometimes help spark new ideas. Change up your team's routine with off-site and walking meetings every now and then. Because it helps to break up the routine, brainstorming at a coffee shop may generate more ideas than you think.

Give people a voice — and follow through on good ideas: Whether anonymously or publicly, it is critical to ensure that people are heard and that they have opportunities to share feedback with one another in order to foster a culture of questioning and challenging ideas. After all, if people don't feel heard or have the opportunity to engage in dialogue, you're going to have a creative deficit in the workplace.

Recognize and reward creativity in the workplace: Recognizing a job well done is essential for keeping people engaged and motivated. And by recognising and rewarding individual and team engagement, you are more likely to be able to foster a creative work environment. As a result, when employees present an idea for a better way to solve a problem, complete a task, or even develop a new product or service, they are rewarded.

Brainstorm: In some ways, project management is nothing more than a never-ending attempt to boost corporate creativity. And brainstorming is a critical component of project management. That is because, as a project manager, you are constantly solving problems – and being creative about them – and, as Richard Branson says, two brains are simply better than one at doing so.

Change must be accommodated, and new technology must be embraced: Many people argue that technology fosters creativity. One of the reasons why technology may be beneficial to creativity is economic convenience. Technology allows you to test your ideas digitally before implementing them in real life, which saves you money and energy.

Provide your team with the appropriate tools (or suites) for creativity: The introduction of time and productivity tracking apps is one of the most recent trends in corporate work environments. The Pomodoro Technique was developed by Francisco Cirillo in the late 1980s to improve his productivity at university, but it has recently gained worldwide popularity.

Organizational Characteristics that Influencing Creativity

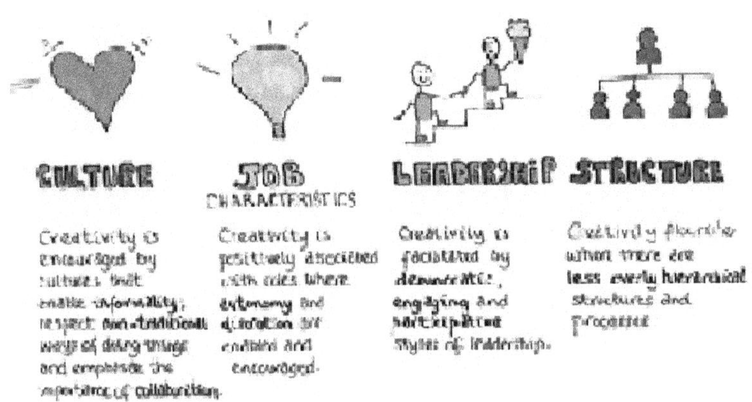

(Amabile, 1983)

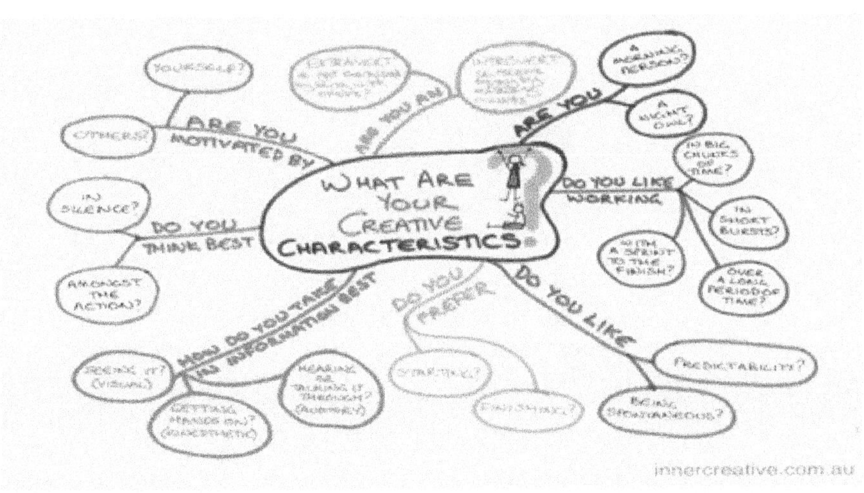

Check your Creative Characteristics

References:

1. Amabile, T. M. (1983). The social psychology of creativity: A componential conceptualization. *Journal of Personality and Social Psychology,* 45(2), 357–376. https://doi.org/10.1037/0022-3514.45.2.357
2. Amabile, T. M. (1983). The Social Psychology of Creativity. New York Springer-Verlag New York
3. The science of creativity. American Psychological Association.
4. Csikszentmihalyi M. *Creativity: Flow and the Psychology of Discovery and Invention.*New York: HarperCollins; 2013.\
5. Kaufman J, Beghetto R. Beyond Big and Little: The Four C Model of Creativity. *Review of General Psychology.* 2009;13(1):1-12. doi:10.1037/a0013688
6. Creativity https://www.csun.edu/~vcpsy00h/creativity/define.htm accessed on 28 June 2021
7. Creativity at workplace https://www.creativityatwork.com/2014/02/17/what-is-creativity/ accessed on 28 June 2021

II

FREUD'S PSYCHOANALYTIC THEORY ON PERSONALITY: FEMINIST APPROACHES ON GENDER CONSTRUCTION

Gurpinder Kumar, Assistant Professor, Centre for Women's Studies, University of Allahabad, Prayagraj, UP-211002, INDIA.

ABSTRACT

Freud's psychoanalytic theory that suggests the gender development occurs in the third stage of psychosexual theory of personality development. Freud called the phallic stage, which occurs between the three-and six-year-old. At this stage, the child's libido is focused on the genitals. The development of gender in the psychoanalytic theory that is different for boys and girls, the boys experience the Oedipus complex, and to identify with their father, and take over the identification of a male role; the girls experience the Electra complex and refer her as identity of her mother as well as tale female gender roles. This paper shows the actual use of the psychoanalytic theory to understand the concept of gender. In the psychoanalytic theory, First, I will describe to you the difference between psychoanalytic theory and other theories of human development, and gender, as well as Freud's contribution to the understanding of gender. Next, I will describe to you the special contributions and changes to the Freudian theory, presented by feminist psychoanalytic theorists in the 1970's and early 1980's. These theories are not only partially corrected, and the sexism in Freud's early theories, but it also made it possible to understand the apparent universality, and the inability of the family. Finally, I will review the more recent feminist psychoanalytic theorists, influenced by postmodernism, queer theory, and the Trans Movement, which argues for the specificity, and the smoothness of the gender, as well as its universality and undesirability.

Keywords: gender, construction, feminism, psychoanalysis,

INTRODUCTION

Freud's psychoanalytic theory, personality develops in stages, each of which is characterized by a certain degree of internal mental conflict. Sigmund Freud ' s psychoanalytic theory of personality argues that human behavior is the result of the interaction of the three parts of the mind: the id, ego and super-ego. This theory is known as Freud's structural theory of personality, which is strongly focused on the role of unconscious psychological conflicts in shaping behavior and personality. The dynamic interactions between the key components of the mind are thought to develop through the use of five different psychosexual stages of development. However, in the last century, Freud's ideas have been the subject of criticism, in part because of his emphasis on sexuality as the most important driver of the development of one's personality. According to Freud, our personality develops as a result of interaction between what is offered in the three most important structures of the human mind: the id, ego and super-ego. The conflict between these three structures, and we strive to have a balance between all of those "desires" to determine how we are to conduct ourselves and how we relate to the world. How do we achieve balance in a given situation, determine how to resolve the conflict between the two different behavioral tendencies; our biological aggressive and pleasure-seeking drives vs. our socialized internal control over those drives.

The Id

The Id is the most primitive of the three structures, is concerned with instant gratification of basic physical needs, and motivations. It works in a completely unconscious (without consciously having to think). For example, if you're *ID* walked past by a stranger consuming ice cream, then, most likely, to have this for itself. It doesn't know, or care, that it would be impolite to accept something that someone else; you are only interested in having that ice cream.

Super-ego

Super-ego is in related to the social principles and moral values which is similar to what a lot of people say it is known as "moral compass". It develops as the child learns what is good and what is bad in the part of their culture. If you're super-ego is passed through the same, or a stranger, he should take out for ice cream, because you knew that it would be rude. However, if you have the id and super-ego are involved, and id be strong enough to overcome your super-ego's fears, on the ice, but after that, you would most likely feel guilty and ashamed for your actions.

The Ego

In distinction to the instinctual id and the moral superego, and the ego is the rational, pragmatic part of our personality. It is less primitive than the id and is partly conscious and partly unconscious. This is what Freud believed that the self and the goal are to balance the demands of the id and the super-ego, in the practical context of the real thing. So, if you walked past the stranger with ice-cream, and your ego is to mediate the conflict between the id (I want to have that ice cream cone now) and the superego (It is wrong to take other people's ice cream), and you decided to buy their own. While this may mean that you will have to wait another 10 minutes, which will hinder your id, your ego, and superego decides to make that sacrifice, as part of a compromise to satisfy his desire for ice cream, or avoidance of an unpleasant social situation, and the potential embarrassment. Freud believed that the id, ego, and superego are in constant conflict, and that adult personality and behavior has its roots in the outcome of this internal conflict during childhood. He believed that a person who has a strong ego, a person, a sound, and a disturbance in the system can lead to neurosis (what we now call anxiety and depression, and unhealthy behaviors.

Psychosexual stages of development

Freud believed that the nature of the conflict between the id, ego and super-ego, changes over time, if a person is changing from a child to an adult. In particular, he argues that such conflicts have to go through a series of stages, each with a different sexual orientation: oral, anal, phallic, latent, and genital. He referred to the idea that the psychosexual theory of development, in which each of the psychosexual stage, which is directly related to the physical center of the fun. Freud's theory of psychosexual development comprises five stages. According to Freud, each stage is carried out in a period of your life. If a person is preoccupied in each of the four stages, he or she develops a personality, according to a certain stage, and the focus. The first stage, the oral stage. The baby at this stage is from birth to eighteen months. The oral phase is focused on the pursuit of pleasure, from the mouth of the baby. At this stage the need for the testing and the related vacuum, visible to the fun. Oral stimulation and it is of paramount importance at this stage as to meet the needs of the child are not met during this time period; the focus will be on the oral stage. A fixation at this stage can result in an adult's habits, such as thumb sucking, smoking, eating too much, and a nail biting. At your age, personal characteristics, are associated with the oral fixation may also occur; these characteristics are optimism, and independence, or the pessimism and hostility. The second stage is the anal stage, which lasts from eighteen months to three years. At this stage, the child's pleasure-seeking centres are located in the intestines, and bladder. During this period, the parents are to pay special attention to the potty training and bowel control. The fixation at the anal stage might lead to anal retentive. Anal retentive characteristics include excessive conscientiousness, accuracy, and good order, while the anal ban is going to disorganization, disorder, and destruction. The third stage is the phallic stage. It begins at the age of three years old, and lasts for up to six. Now the sensitivity is focused on the genitals, masturbation (for both sexes) is a new source of pleasure. The child will begin to understand the anatomical differences between men and women, which have led to a sense of jealousy and fear, which Freud called the Oedipus complex (in boys). Later, the Freudian scholars are added to the Electra complex (in girls). The fourth stage is that of the secret place, starting at the age of six, and it will run until the end, but maybe not. At this stage, not a single part of your body and looking to have fun instead of all of the sexual feelings are repressed. In this way, children can develop social skills, and comfort in social interactions with peers and family members. In the final stage of psychosexual development is the genital stage. This stage begins at the age of eleven, and continues up to the age of puberty, and ends when a person reaches adulthood at the age of eighteen years of age. The onset of puberty, which reflects a person's strong interest in a person to other opposite sexes. If a person does not have experience with the consent of the psychosexual stages, the reach of the genital stage, they will have a well-balanced person.

Criticism of Freud's theory

Even though Freud's theories have a number of advantages that have contributed to the expansion of our psychological understanding of personality, and they are not open-ended. The focus is on the structure of human consciousness, Freud's little attention has been paid to the influence of the environment, the social sciences or the world. His theories were strongly committed to the region, and to a large extent ignored the "normal" healthy effect. He has also been criticized for his narrow minded attitude to human sexuality, to the exclusion of other important factors. Many critics point out that Freud's theories are not supported by the empirical (experimental) evidence. In fact, when scientists began to examine his ideas of a more scientifically, it has become clear that some of them could not be confirmed that a theory is scientific, it needs to be able to rule out ("forge"), as well as the experimental evidence, and many of Freud's ideas are not falsifiable. It is worth pointing out, and contemporary critics have been very critical of many of Freud's theories, which seems to indicate that the accounting policies and methods of psychoanalytic theory, is deeply patriarchal (male-dominated), and anti-feminist, and misogynistic (anti-women). Karen Horney, a psychologist, traveled to Freud, they believed that the "Freudian approach as a foundation, "the male one." Feminist Betty Friedan referred to Freud's concept of penis envy" is purely a social bias that is typical of the Victorian era, and demonstrates how this concept played a crucial role in discrediting alternative ideas regarding the female in the beginning and in the middle of the twenty-first century.

Neo-Freudian approaches to personality

Even though Sigmund Freud was an important contribution to the field of psychology, it is thanks to his psychoanalytic theory of personality; his work was not well studied. Many people have made criticisms of his theories, the focus is on issues of sexuality; and, in the years that have passed, it is his work, and many, many other researchers have tweaked and developed his ideas for the creation of a new theory of the personality. This is the neo-Freudian theorists generally agreed with Freud that childhood experiences were important, but they have reduced the emphasis on sex and sexuality. Instead of a strictly biological approach to the development of personality, such as Freud did, by focusing on the individual, the evolutionary gestures), they focus more holistically on how the social context and culture impact on the individual's development. A lot of psychologists, scientists, and philosophers have made significant additions to the psychoanalytic studies of the personality. The four most well-known neo-Freudians include Alfred Adler, Erik Erikson, Carl Jung and Karen Horney.

Alfred Adler

Alfred Adler was the first to explore the development of a comprehensive social, psychodynamic theory of personality. He founded a school of psychology called individual psychology, which focuses on what we need to do in order to compensate for feelings of inferiority. Adler introduced the concept of the inferiority complex, that is, how a person's feelings that they don't matter, and does not conform to the standards of others or of the community. He, too, believed in the importance of social relations, in view of the fact that the child will be considered during the development of the social development, on the site of the sexual phase, described by Freud. On the basis of these ideas, Amenities and identifies three important tasks that all of us have to solve are: occupational tasks (careers), social (friendship), and love tasks (such as finding a partner for a long-term relationship.

Eric Erickson

Erik Erikson is best-known for the proposal of the psycho-social theory of development, in which it is assumed that a person's personality develops over a lifetime, on the basis of social relationships, and a departure from Freud's biology is focused on the view. In his psychological theory, Erickson emphasized the social relationships, which is the case in each of the stages of development of the personality, in contrast to Freud, who stresses the need to have sex. Erickson has identified eight stages, each of which is a dispute or a challenge. The development of a healthy personality and a sense of competence are subject to the successful completion of each task.

Carl Jung

Carl Jung is followed by Adler's footsteps, to the development of a theory of personality, in which analytical psychology, it is concerned. One of Jung's most important contributions was the concept of the collective unconscious, which he regarded as Freud's, as the "universal" version of the personal unconscious mental patterns, or memory traces, which are common to all of us (Jung, 1928). These ancestral memories, which, Jungian archetypes, are represented by the universal themes expressed in terms of the art and literature of the different cultures, as well as the dreams of the people. Jung introduced the concept of the persona, which refers to a kind of "mask" that is what we have on the basis of our experience, and in this course, as it is in our collective unconscious. Jung believed that the person is acting as a trade-off between who we really are (our true self) and the society expect from us; we hide behind a mask, which can be the parts of ourselves that do not meet up to the expectations of the society.

Karen Horney

Karen Horney was one of the first women to be trained as a Freudian psychoanalyst. Karen Horney's theories have focused on the "unconscious anxiety", which, she believed, came from the early childhood experiences, needs and challenges, of loneliness and / or isolation. Karen theorized the three styles of coping that they take in relation to fear of movement in the direction of people, moving away from the people and for the movement of people. Karen Horney was also a major influence on the development of feminism in the field of psychodynamics. To Freud, it is often criticized for the installation of almost all men for what some see as a retreat for the women; for example, Horney disagreed with the Freudian idea that the girls are jealous of the penis, and is jealous of the men of biological functions. According to Horney, each and every blind is the most likely to the level of permissions that are often people who have it, which means that the differences between men's and women's personalities emerge from the dynamics of culture, not of biology. Furthermore, it suggests that men experience womb envy" because they don't have.

Gender-based socialization

One way to interpret that Beauvoir's declaration of a person is not born, but becomes, a woman has to take it as an indication of the socialization of gender, females become women, and the processes by which they are acquiring female characteristics, and learn how women's behavior. It is believed that masculinity and femininity is the product of the nurse or the nursing units. They may be causally structured (Haslanger, 1995), social forces have a main playing role in the development of the gender of the individuals, and (in some sense) to shape the way in which they become, women, and men. The mechanism of the activities of social learning. For example, Kate Millett, is of the opinion that the gender differences between men and women above all, the cultural rather than the biological foundation, which is the result of a variety of relationships, (Millet, 1971). For her, gender is the fullness of your parents, peers, and culture, the perception of what is appropriate for one's gender, temperament, personality, interests, status, dignity, a gesture and a word (Millett 1971). Male-and-female-gender-norms, however, are a problem in the generation of behavior that fits comfortably in the subordination of women, and to ensure that women are socialized in a subordinate role in society, they are taught to be passive, ignorant, easy-going, emotional, machines for men. However, because these roles are to be taken into account, we can create a more equal society, and "unlearning" of social roles. That is, women should aim to reduce the impact of socialization. Social learning theorists believe that there are such a lot of different influences that is to socialize us, women as well as men. In this case, it's very hard to stand up to gender socialization. For example, parents are often unaware of the treatment for male and female children differently. When parents were asked to describe it, it is available 24 hours a day for the kids, and they were, therefore, the use of gender-stereotyped language, the boys are described as strong, alert, and in a consistent manner, and the girls are described as " a small, soft, and tender. Parents ' attitudes toward their children will also give the descriptions, whether they are aware of it or not (Renzetti & Curran 1992). Some of socialization, it is even more pronounced: the children are often dressed up in a sex-stereotyped clothing and colors, the boys are dressed in blue and girls in pink, and the parents tend to buy their children's gender-stereotyped toys and games. They also have the tendency to (intentionally or not), and to strengthen some of the "good" behavior. Although the precise form of the socialization of the sexes has changed a lot since the arrival of the second wave of feminism, and even today, girls are not encouraged to play sports, such as football, or playing the "rough and tumble" of the game, and they are more likely than boys to the doll or other accessories, toys to play-the boys are told not to "cry like a baby" and give men's toys such as cars and guns. According to the theories of social learning, children will also have an impact on what we see in the world. This makes it more difficult to counter gender socialization. First of all, in the books of the children, men and women are represented in real life stereotypes, for example, men, women, and leaders, as well as the women's assistant and the students. One of the best ways to deal with gender stereotyping in children's books, and was the portrayal of women in an independent role, while the men were not aggressive, and health care (Renzetti & Curran 1992). Some publishers have attempted to use an alternative approach, which makes their characters-for example, gender neutral, animals, or asexual imaginary creatures, (such as the teletubbies on TV). However, the parents in the book, of gender-neutral or genderless characters are often undermining the publishers of the efforts made by them to read with their children in such a way that the characters are either male or female. According to Renzetti and Curran, parents are called, and the vast majority of those are gender-neutral, male characters, such as characters, that are compatible with the female gender stereotypes (such as good) and were referred to as a woman (Renzetti & Curran, 1992). The interacting effects of these are thought to have implicit messages about how men and women should behave, and it is expected that you will work through us, created in both female and male personalities.

Psychoanalytic feminism

Psychoanalytic feminism is the theory of grief, which states that men have a psychological need to submit to women. The roots of the men's desire for dominance over women, and women with the minimum of resistance, and the submission to lie deep within the human psyche. This branch of feminism that strives to gain knowledge about how the life of a reason to evolve in order to better understands it and to change it, the oppression of women. The model reduction is also integrated in the society, and the creation and maintenance of patriarchy. With the help of psychoanalytic methods in order to examine the differences between men and women, as well as ways to build the gender, you can reorganize the socialization of the models are in the early stages of the human life. Social change or "cure" may be made by the open-source of the complete dominance in the male psyche, and submission of the female psyche and that is largely unnoticed, in the ignorance of the people.

Psychoanalysis and feminism

"The Second Sex" by Simon de Beauvoir (1949), and "The Feminine Mystique" by Betty Friedan (1963), both theorized psychoanalysis as stated women as being inferior, and defined only in relation to men. Then, in the 1970s, a second wave of feminist works, such as Kate Millet's Sexual Politics (1970) The Dialectic of Sex by Shulamith Firestone (1970), and Germaine Greer's The Female Eunuch (1970), has called for changes in the society, which is helping to tackle sexual inequality. Mitchell's book, Psychoanalysis and Feminism (1972), was an important milestone in the revival of the analysis, and the interpretation of the revolutionary concept of the women. As of the start of the analysis, the argument is that the physical reality of the race is to be distinguished from the anatomical fact, that there is no clear correlation between the fields of biology and psychology. Men and women have been physically or socially "made" as men or the women, but they become such. Initially, however, as Freud assumed, a symmetry in the development of what he called the Oedipus complex. Alone, in an essay written in 1925, it was for Freud, a distinction should be made between the psychosexual history of the boys and girls, and recognizing the importance of the pre-oedipal phase, in which the boys and girls, for the love of the mother, and the two have to abandon her in favor of the father (1925). A young girl with the love of her mother, her father, and it is as if a man wants to be a mother, in the sense that, later on, his wife. In this model, the boys identify with their fathers, and because of their masculine identity are determined. A boy learns of his role as a father, the heir. The girl, on the other hand, has to be able to identify with the mother, while at the same time, a rejection of her as an object of love, the love, object and turning to her father instead.

According to Freud, the date of the rejection by the mother, it is based on the frustration, and the frustration that is not able to meet her mother's, and it goes hand in hand with the enemy. The importance of pre oedipal relationship a mother has been fully discussed, since Freud's time. Recently, interest in the nature of a female's personality is reflected in the works of Ethel Guy, Irene, Soon, and Jessica Benjamin, and in the United States, as well as in the work of Janine Chasseguet-Smirgel, Catherine J., and Jean-Parat, Marie, and Toroc, and Joyce McDougall in France. In the 1920's, a controversy broke out on the perception of femininity. If Freud's libido, it is the same for both sexes; it is, in the English language school by the female sex drive is. Karen Horney and Ernest Jones who took part in a series of exchanges, and argued against Freud's view of the making of a "positive" image of women's sexuality is distinct from the concept of the provision of services. For Jones, the evolution of the female is associated with a physical constitution. In a legal dispute with him, as well as Freud pointed out that he deeply understood the basic nature of the sexuality, and that he had been restored to the biological reductionism. Mitchell said that, in the Freud - Jones, the controversy has shifted to the question of the differences between men and women, on what is specific to each gender. The development of the psychoanalytic theory in the UK, along with the school of objects relations, and lead to a focus on the parent-child dyad and the role of motherhood. Psychoanalytic work from the early focusing on the poor conditions in the early stages, and gradually, the attention is focused on the impact of the poor conditions at the time of transfer. Melanie Klein's theory continued to Freud, the shift of emphasis from the father, the mother, and the importance of a mother to the children of both sexes. In front of her, and the relationship of the child to the mother's body has been described above, the emotional life. In particular, the breast is a ratio; it is of crucial importance in a child's early experiences. Klein's concept of the instructive, and projective identification, are metaphors for the body of the processes of the absorption of the movement. According to Klein, it's a little girl who believes that her mother's body has everything it needs, including those of her father's penis. The result of this is a girl who is full of hatred for her mother, and wants to attack you and rob you of the inside of the body. After that, she filled out due to the fear of being "having the inside of her body robbed and destroyed." In 1928, the Small, pointed out that it is in the chest, discomfort, and it is not the discovery of the lack of a penis, the girl away from her mother to her father.

Later on, she played down the child of the first one breast, jealousy, envy, and he wrote specifically about heterosexual attraction to young girls. A small view of the early mother-child relationship, and the effect of some earlier work on the subject of femininity in society, more reasonable approach is to start with the investment by the funds in advance so that you are prepared for the purpose. Progressive psychoanalysts from all sections of British society, and was inspired by the work of Klein, Donald Winnicott, Marjorie Brierly, and Wilfred Bion, which emphasizes the connection between the primary emotional development, and object relationships. These patterns can be found in the writings of Marion Burgner Pink and Adcumbe, Aigle Laufer, Dinora Pines, Said Brin, Joan Raphael-Leff, and Rosina Perelberg. In a later collection, this is found in the work of the three schools of psycho-analysis in the British Psychoanalytical Society, and Raphael-Leff, and Perelberg emphasis primal connection to the mother, and for her appearances in the transference and counter transference. American feminists believe that the analysis provides a patriarchal inequality. Nancy Chodorrow is one of the best-known writers in the United States, on the connection between psycho-analysis and feminism. The Reproduction of Mothering: Psychoanalysis and the Sociology of Gender (1978) introduced American readers to the work of the Winnicott, W. Ronald Fairbairn, and Harry Gantrip. Chodorow stresses on development in relation to the others, with a focus on the pre-Oedipal relationship between mother and child.

They will have the function of being a mother to an asymmetric relationship between the boys and the girls. Girl has more permeable boundaries in your relationships with others and, as a result of the fact that she's a mother, a person of the same sex. Why do girls and women are more devoted to being a mother. The boys, on the contrary, they will develop a sense of self-esteem, in contrast to the mother, and to set more stringent limits. Men's perceptions of themselves are more spread out. Jean Baker Miller, and Carol Gilligan, of the School of inter-personal Analysis to emphasize the feminine traits of a relationship, moved to pity, and to make sure that it can be considered to be a decline in a male-dominated culture. These interpersonal theorists emphasize the cultural focus on the different characteristics of men and women, and the focus is less on the inner world of unconscious fantasies, and the internal object relations. Jessica Benjamin in the "Bond of Love" (1988) and, see both, boys, and girls looking for their father, and to confirm it. While the boy's identity is confirmed by the father, the girl in contrast has her identification with the father's power denied, and he becomes the object of her ideal ego. This will prevent her from having a "will of its own, and her desire for her father to be tinge with masochism, issues of power and submission in the sphere of relationships. Chodorow, the argument is that what all these authors have in common, despite their differences, the strain on their sites as "not applicable" (or the non-acceptance of the relationship). She argues that this position is an abrupt break with the essentialist view of gender, and is moving in the direction of the view that, by default, masculinity and femininity, in order relationally constructed context. These schools, but in the end, the building of a more stable view of femininity and masculinity than Earlier, which is, in principle, to the fact that there is a flow between masculinity and femininity in both men and women. These features can be compared with the latest trends in the French theories of psychoanalysis, and feminism, which is to emphasize unconscious fantasies, and desires, and try to find a language for the expression of the feminine principle. Below are the French psychoanalysts, in particular, there is an opinion that the "discovery" of the unconscious is, in itself, does not reveal the fact that the person is in a state of fantasy and desire. This is a radical perspective in the analysis can provide with feminism. The impact of the work of Jacques Lacan, permeates much of the work of those who accept the postulates of Freudian theory, and to those who, like Julia Kristeva, Helene Sixus, Michel Montreulet, Sarah Kofman, and Luce Irigaray continued to be very critical for the analysis of the basic assumptions. Lacan pointed out, that is, the difference between the penis and the phallus, it is fundamental to Freud's distinction between the biological and psychological reality. The phallus is the anatomical reality; it is a symbol of the mother's desire. Joel Dor suggested that the central question of the Oedipus complex, and it is, therefore, "to be or not to be the phallus," which is to say, to be or not to be to the object of her desire. The role of the father is symbolic; it represents the possibility of the object of their desire. The phallus, as opposed to penis enlargement, it is of no one (neither male nor female, and is a combination of the two genders. Chasseguet-Smirgel, McDougall, Torok, Luquet Parat, Monique Cournet-Jeannin, and Jacqueline Schaeffer have all said, from the point of view of psycho-analysis. Chasseguet-Smirgel pointed out, in her perception, the fact that the girl knew about the existence of a vagina, almost from the beginning, though, she suggests that the "know-how" that can be ruled out, the unconscious, what is the girl, well knows, and you don't know. Some of his works, "penis envy" is defined as having a protective role. For many of the French feminist writers, and the body is the locus of the female, as well as a range of work that tries to capture it in its rhythms, In her book," Speculum " (1974), Irigaray explores the psycho-analysis as an awareness of the historical and philosophical determinants of the private discourse, and the analysis of their own unconscious fantasies. In addition, being a product of a patriarchal society, it can analyze what it owes to the mother. She constantly puts herself in the position where women don't have any personal identify. She emphasizes the girl by her mother's body. The girl, says Irigaray , has the mother, in a sense, in her skin, the wetness of its mucous membrane, in the vicinity of what is most intimate to share, it is in the mystery of her posture, pregnancy, childbirth, and sexual identity. Kristeva links of spiritual suppression, the real structure of the language, and describes the pre oedipal stage, as a play of the body's rhythms, and to pre linguistic exchange between the child and the child's mother. Kristeva refers to that which Plato, in the Timaeus, called the chora as the site of the undifferentiated bodily space the mother and the child share. Inside the Oedipus complex that is dominated by the last of the unified text, or cultural knowledge. This is the difference between the semiotic and the symbolic, in retrospect, for it is only by means of a symbolic of a person to have access to the semiotic. For For Kristeva, subjectivity is founded on a constitutive repression of the maternal, the chora, the semiotic, and the abject (liminal states, like pregnancy). Kristeva has been accused of leading women, a mother's job, but it is also seen as a way in order to have a better understanding on pre oedipal.. Interestingly enough, if you go back to Freud's concept of hysteria. The occurrence of the first psychoanalytic patient, Anna O., included mutism, paralysis, "time-missing," and gaps in memory: all expressing interruptions in the domain of a reality which is being denied. Psychoanalysis indicates that sexuality is only created through division and discontinuity, although femininity is the side that both represents, and tends to be represented as, the negative (of masculinity).

CONCLUSION

In the analysis, is a critical diagnostic project, you do not necessarily have the legislative or policy. Due to the development of a theory of motivation, and the non-rational forces that move and inspire us, and the idea that we are opaque rather than transparent, to ourselves, and not be able to fully self-knowledge or self-control, and psychoanalytic theory, it also challenges the rational, the human ego, and it shows that the ethical character of political and community may not be perfect, find the uncertainty in both the spiritual and political identity. Please do not assume that the unconscious is by a transgressive, or a conservative, but it is unreliable, sometimes it is beneficial for the rebellion or a rebellion, which was a strong and determined to defend the borders. Even though they are often in a complex environment and the psychoanalytic description of the unconscious and offer a feminist resource theory in both the political and the ontological investigation. Ontologically, the analysis shows a clear mental concept of, and the differences between men and women, and how we can live in our body and of our personality, and falsely informed the analysis, which is not reducible to either the social or the other of the categories. From a political point of view, the analysis provides a description of the forces, that will organize, disorganize, and the order of the relationship that the two of us. By providing insight into the formation of subjectivity, and animating fantasies, make use of the social life, the normal use, so it will also be the failure of the analysis of the enduring elements of a patriarchal social relations, including symbolic links, and the internal forces are used to support the identity, and the terminals of the sexual participants are in a relationship of domination and submission. Psychoanalytic feminism, and focus on the most important component of the society, the core of the differences between men and women in the community, helping to explain the final stage of male power, and enables feminist theorists to articulate possible correctives, problems, and ways to improve it, or ethical violations that are returned to politics and beyond, and not only in terms of the work to the public sphere.

REFERENCES

- Benjamin, Jessica. (1988). *Bond's Of Love*, United Kingdom: AwesomeBooks
- Chodorow, Nancy. (1978). *The Reproduction of Mothering: Psychoanalysis and the Sociology of Gender*, University of California Press.
- De Beauvoir, S. (1949). *The Second Sex*, Harmondsworth: Penguin Books Ltd.
- Firestone, Shulamith. (1970). *The Dialectic of Sex: The Case for Feminist Revolution*. New York: William Morrow and Company.
- Friedan, B. (1963). *Feminine Mystique*, Harmondsworth: Penguin Books Ltd.
- Freud, Sigmund. (1905). *Three Essays on the Theory of Sexuality*, London: Imago Publishing
- Greer, Germaine. (1970). *The Female Eunuch*, United Kingdom: MacGibbon & Kee
- Haslanger, S. (1995). "Ontology and Social Construction", *Philosophical Topics*, 23: 95–125.
- Hooks, Bell. (2000). *Feminist Theory: From Margins to Center*, London: Pluto Press.
- Jaggar, Alison. (1983) "Human Biology in Feminist Theory: Sexual Equality Reconsidered", in *Beyond Domination: New Perspectives on Women and Philosophy*, C. Gould (ed.), Lanham: Rowman & Littlefield Publishers, Inc.
- Jung, Carl. (1928). *Two Essays on Analytical Psychology* (1st ed). London: Routledge.
- Millett, Kate. (1970). *Sexual Politics*, London: Granada Publishing Ltd.
- Mitchell, Juliet. (1972). *Psychoanalysis and feminism*. UK: Penguin Books.
- Raphael-Leff, Joan, and Perelberg, Rosine Jozef (Eds.) (1997). *Female experience: Three generations of British women psychoanalysts on work with women*. London: Routledge.
- Renzetti, C. and D. Curran (1992). "Sex-Role Socialization", in *Feminist Philosophies*, J. Kourany, J. Sterba, and R. Tong (eds.), New Jersey: Prentice Hall.
- Rogers, L. (1999). *Sexing the Brain*, London: Phoenix.
- Wright, Elizabeth. (1992). *Feminism and psychoanalysis: A critical dictionary*. Oxford, UK: Blackwell.

- H. G. Baynes and C. F. Baynes. 1928. *Contributions to Analytical Psychology*, London: Routledge.

• 24 •

III

UNDERSTANDING AND MANAGING DISRUPTIVE BEHAVIOR IN ADOLESCENTS

Dr.Mukta Goyal,*Assistant Professor, Guru Nanak Dev. Institute of Technology, Delhi.*
Department of management,

INTRODUCTION

Adolescence is frequently associated with behavioural issues. Student disruption, aggression, and academic failure are widespread issues in schools across the country. Adolescence is a time when people learn to be self-sufficient. Adolescents typically assert their independence by questioning or challenging, and sometimes breaking, rules. Parents and doctors must distinguish between isolated instances of poor judgment and a pattern of misbehaviour that necessitates professional intervention. The severity and frequency of infractions serve as indicators. Regular drinking, frequent episodes of fighting, absenteeism without permission (truancy), and theft, for example, are far more serious than isolated episodes of the same activities. Other warning signs include poor academic performance and running away from home. Adolescents who cause serious injury or use a weapon in a fight are of particular concern.

Adolescents are often out of the direct physical control of adults because they are much more independent and mobile than children were. Adolescents' behaviour is governed by their own moral and behavioural code in these circumstances. Parents' guide rather than directly control their children's behaviour. Adolescents who feel loved and supported by their parents are less likely to engage in risky behaviour. Adolescents whose parents communicate clear expectations about their children's behaviour are also more likely to succeed.

Authoritarian parenting is a parenting style in which children help to set family expectations and rules. This parenting style is more likely to promote mature behaviours than authoritarian parenting (in which parents make decisions with little input from their children) or permissive parenting (in which parents set few limits).

- Authoritarian parenting employs a system of graduated privileges in which adolescents are first given small amounts of responsibility (such as caring for a pet, doing household chores, purchasing clothing, decorating their room, or managing an allowance). When adolescents handle a responsibility or privilege well over time, more responsibilities and privileges are granted, such as going out with friends without parents and driving. Poor judgment or a lack of responsibility, on the other hand, results in the loss of privileges. Each new privilege necessitates close parental supervision to ensure that adolescents follow the agreed-upon rules.
- **Disruptive behaviour,** which is more common in males, is clinically significant behaviour that disrupts the adolescent's interpersonal context. Adolescents who exhibit disruptive behaviour lack the ability to self-regulate affect and behaviour, which is required for social adaptation. This self-regulation deficit is shaped by biological vulnerability (e.g. Temperament, genetics), as well as the regulating and developmental influence of family function.
- Adolescence is the time when a person transitions from childhood to adulthood. It involves significant physical and psychological changes in a young person's life. ... Understanding what to expect at different stages of adolescence and early adulthood might help to encourage healthy development.

Externalizing Adolescent Problem Behaviors

- Externalizing Adolescent Problem Behaviors such as Delinquent behavior, Aggression, and Adult Crime Later Adolescence has been viewed as a developmental stage in the individual's life. Across studies conducted in the 1990s, there has been an increase in the prevalence of both internalizing and externalizing disorders among youth. Externalizing problem behaviors are generally demonstrated to be a robust finding (Keil& Price, 2006).
- Moffitt (1993) defines formalized among cross-sectional studies, two general types of adolescent problem behavior as clinically relevant externalizing behavior problems, i.e. overtly aggressive behavior, are described along the two dimensions.
- Dimensions such as inhibition versus aggression (Miller, 1967), over controlled versus empirically based multivariate studies (Frick, Lahey, Loeber; under controlled (Achenbach & Edelbrock, 1978), or internalizing Tannenbaum, Van Horn, Christ, 1993 have been identified. Relationships with internalizing versus externalizing issues (Achenbach, 1966; 1991). It has also been discovered that antisocial peers are related to the
- Aggression and juvenile delinquency are typical examples of externalizing behavior emergence (Elliott, Huizinger, &Ageton, externalizing problem behavior. Internalizing behavioral issues (1985), particularly when these relationships are strained.

Adolescence is recognised by the World Health Organization (WHO) and the United Nations as the period between the ages of 10 and 19.

- Adolescence is a period of growth and development. The existence or absence of a number of intervening and moderating influences and contextual elements will invariably determine whether adolescents' life meaning and wisdom will grow and unfold from being relatively straightforward to being mature and complex. The complete absence of these moderating forces may stifle the development of personal meaning, but their partial presence may promote and even expedite the search for personal meaning in life among teenagers. Both personal meaning and wisdom are seen to have their origins in interpersonal relationships and social transactions during adolescence, requiring teenagers to engage in discussion and discourse with peers and other reference groups. According to studies, 30% of adolescents wish to work in a field that allows them to make a positive difference in the world.

Adolescents who had purposeful job goals also reported higher meaning in their lives and schooling, according to regression analysis. Adolescence, on the other hand, is often connected with puberty and the cycle of physical changes that leads to reproductive maturity in many countries. In other cultures, adolescence is defined in broader terms that include psychological, social, and moral components of maturation as well as the strictly physical aspects. Adolescence is marked by an increase in abstract thinking, knowledge, and logical reasoning skills.

- This is when the majority of behavioural issues arise. The types of problems vary depending on the child's age and might encompass a wide range of issues. Adolescents are particularly vulnerable to mental illnesses.

Adolescence is characterised by a great deal of emotional and behavioural upheaval. While adhering to conventional rules, the adolescent fights to create his uniqueness. They have been exposed to societal changes as a result of rapid urbanisation and modernisation. The teenager is more vulnerable to dysfunctional thinking and behaviour as a result of the collapse in family structure and excessive or insufficient control. The proper resolution of these emotional and behavioural issues is necessary for adulthood to be healthy. Most adolescents successfully navigate this tightrope and reach adulthood. Not every adolescent will be lucky enough to receive the necessary societal support for a successful transition. Some people acquire maladaptive emotional and behavioural tendencies. This portends a bleak future for the individual, leading in sadness, delinquency, and suicide, among other issues. Adolescents are experiencing an increase in the prevalence of mental illness and maladaptive behaviours. According to WHO estimates, up to 20% of adolescents have one or more mental or behavioural issues. Adolescents with behavioural and emotional difficulties are shown to be prevalent in 16.5 percent to 40.8 percent of the time, according to studies conducted around the world. 6 and in India, it ranges from 13.7 percent to 50 percent. Adolescents account for one-fifth of India's population, implying a significant disease burden on the country. According to a literature analysis, the prevalence rate of emotional and behavioural issues among teenagers in India ranges from 13.7% to 50%. According to research, 75% of adolescents who thought they were performing poorly academically actually had behavioural/emotional issues. 43 percent of teenagers who believed their parents were dissatisfied with their academic performance developed the mental health problem mentioned above. Adolescents' emotional and behavioural problems were found to be linked to parental disagreement. Inter-parental conflict has been found to be a significant predictor of adolescent suicide. Family ties are an essential protective factor in war-affected adolescents that needs to be investigated further by gender.

Adolescence is a time when people learn to be self-sufficient.

- Adolescents usually demonstrate their independence by questioning or challenging rules, and perhaps breaking them. Parents and doctors must be able to tell the difference between an occasional lapse in judgement and a pattern of misbehaviour that necessitates professional intervention. Infractions' severity and frequency serve as indicators. Regular drinking, frequent fights, truancy (absenteeism without permission), and stealing, for example, are all significantly more serious than isolated incidents of the same behaviour. Other warning indicators include a drop in academic performance and a desire to flee the house. Adolescents who cause serious injury or use a weapon in a fight are of particular concern.

Adolescents are often out of the direct physical control of parents because they are considerably more autonomous and mobile than youngsters.

- Adolescents' behaviour is dictated by their own moral and behavioural code in these situations. Parents should guide rather than direct their children's actions. Parents who provide warmth and support to their children are less likely to engage in dangerous behaviour. Adolescents who have clear expectations for their behaviour and who have constant limit setting and monitoring from their parents are less likely to participate in dangerous behaviours. An alarming proportion of our teenagers suffer from emotional and behavioural issues that have their origins in the home.
- Then there are sleep issues, which are widespread in adolescence and have a severe impact on adolescents' mental health and functioning. Biological rhythms varies from person to person. Some people are morning people, preferring intellectual and physical activity in the morning, while others are evening people. There were links between

this morningness-eveningness construct and several elements of mental health and well-being; for example, eveningness was linked to depression and seasonal affective disorders.

- **Adolescents who have more evenings have more challenges**.
- Eveningness and sleeplessness are both frequent in adolescents, but it's unclear if they have a separate or combined effect on the likelihood of psychopathology. Evening-type teenagers were more likely to experience insomnia symptoms. Evenings and insomnia were found to be independently linked to an increased risk of emotional and behavioural issues. Eveningness and sleeplessness symptoms are both risk factors for adolescent mental illness. When analysing and treating psychopathology in adolescents, it's important to include both sleep and circadian aspects. Boys were twice as likely as girls to break the rules or engage in delinquent behaviour. Adolescents have become increasingly accustomed to consuming energy drinks. Boys and older teens were more likely to consume energy drinks on a regular basis. Adolescents from middle-income families were less likely to consume energy drinks on a regular basis. Adolescents who used energy drinks on a daily basis had greater health and behavioural issues, as well as less positive school experiences. When researchers looked at the relationship between various socio-environmental factors and emotional and behavioural problems in adolescents, they discovered that children whose parents were addicted to alcohol or illicit drugs had up to three times as many behavioural and emotional problems as children whose parents were not addicted.

Alcoholism was discovered to be the most common addiction,

- with adolescents from addicted households having a threefold higher frequency of behavioural and emotional difficulties. Young people whose parents were alcoholics were more likely to seek help from friends and siblings than from their parents. Cigarette smoking was found to be highly linked to greater levels of emotional and behavioural issues. The emotional/behavioral health of adolescents may be useful in the creation of effective anti-smoking programmes in the classroom and elsewhere. Globally, chronic diseases and disorders are on the rise. An ageing population and socioeconomic changes are contributing to a continuous rise in these prevalent and expensive long-term health issues.

Adolescents with chronic illnesses have also been found to be significantly linked to problems. Asthma and other chronic respiratory tract diseases, musculoskeletal issues, and heart disease are the most frequent of these conditions. Adolescents are more prone than healthy controls to acquire mental and behavioural disorders, have a greater incidence of at least one psychiatric diagnosis, and are depressed or have low self-esteem.

Adolescents with a history of physical abuse were nearly twice as likely to have behavioural and emotional issues.

- Abused children had a seven-fold increased risk of developing a serious depressive condition. Abused boys were shown to have the same risk of getting depression as abused girls. The mechanism by which an increase in life stress can lead to emotional and behavioural disorders in adolescents is through negative automatic thinking. Adolescents from refugee and migrant families may be at a higher risk of developing emotional and behavioural issues. Migrant teenagers have had more traumatic experiences and have more peer issues and avoidance behaviours. Non-migrant teenagers, on the other hand, show higher anxiety, externalising difficulties, and hyperactivity. The frequency of traumatic experiences experienced, gender, and living condition are all factors that influence the prevalence of emotional and behavioural issues. Although the prevalence of emotional and behavioural symptoms in migrant and non-migrant adolescents is similar, special attention should be paid to the screening and support of vulnerable groups within the migrant population, such as girls, those who have experienced numerous traumatic events, and unaccompanied refugee children and adolescents. Adolescents with behavioural issues had a more negative assessment of the environment when it came to most of the variables linked to family, school, and peers. Clearly, behavioural issues are linked to issues in a variety of settings. Multiple regression analyses revealed that problems at school were the most important predictor of behavioural problem scores for boys, whereas problems at home were the most important predictor of behavioural problem scores for girls. Furthermore, living in a disadvantaged neighbourhood is linked to more behavioural issues, which may worsen as children transition from childhood to adolescent. The neighbourhood environment must be included in public health programmes to improve child mental health. Furthermore, consistent genetic affects were detected throughout ages, demonstrating that genetic factors exhibited as early as age 4 years support biological basis underlying adolescent behavioural disorders. At each age, however, genetic and environmental changes were detected. This suggests that while genetic variables are crucial for understanding stable individual differences in behavioural disorders across childhood and adolescence, fresh genetic effects can also help transform such behaviours. Higher levels of physical activity and a higher parental socioeconomic status were linked to better overall academic achievement and future goals for higher education in fully adjusted models. High behavioural problem scores were associated with inferior overall academic achievement and future academic intentions. In conclusion, higher levels of physical activity, less behavioural difficulties, and a higher socioeconomic status were all linked to high self-perceived overall academic performance and plans for higher education among adolescents. The interrelationships of these elements, as well as the beneficial link between physical activity, mental health, and school results, provide a vital backdrop for future research, intervention programming, and policy aimed at enhancing adolescent educational attainment. While emotional and behavioural issues put youth's development at risk, resilience allows them to adapt and overcome adversity.

DISRUPTIVE BEHAVIOUR COMPONENTS

- Disruptive behaviour is a component of many disorders, but a disease model does not fully explain it. Descriptive diagnostic statements provide clinicians with information about what youth do. They do not, however, explain why the behaviour occurs, nor do they outline treatments to manage the behaviour. In order to do so, one must look to the emerging field of developmental psychopathology and the impact of family function on self-regulation.
- Some of the most problematic externalizing behaviours are lying, stealing, vandalism, truancy, arson, promiscuity, defiance toward authority, disinhibit ion (severe impulsivity), and aggression (threatening, bullying, fighting, rape).Reasons for seeing a child and adolescent psychiatrist Outside of the family, such as schoolmates and

teachers, the disruptive behaviour may pose a problem.

- The psychiatric evaluation of children with disruptive behaviour follows the standard evaluation format, with special areas of investigation for the disruptive adolescent (Table 1). The first step in making a treatment decision is to collect detailed psychiatric and medical histories from both the adolescent and his or her family. A neuropsychological/psychological evaluation, brain imaging (MRI, CT), or electroencephalography are examples of additional assessments.
- Those who have been impacted by the adolescent's disruptive behaviour (Parents, classmates, and extended family) provide critical information such as age of onset, type of behaviour (e.g., aggressive), and precipitating factors. As a result, the clinician can evaluate the interactional component: Who is impacted? Where does the disruption happen? When does it usually happen?
- It is critical to observe the interaction between the parent(s) and the adolescent. A parent's harshness, inconsistency, or indulgence can have a significant impact on their child's behaviour. A mental status examination that assesses intellectual ability and communication skills, aggressive/homicidal ideation, paranoia or other psychotic symptoms, and empathy capacity should also be included in the evaluation. Treatment sequencing for adolescent disruptive behaviour.
- In the treatment of disruptive youth, interventions should be integrated or sequenced.
- This proposed sequence includes some early family and parent work to disrupt individual symptom-maintaining family interactions, without which individual work fails:

- Use pharmacology and parent management training to stabilize behaviour.
- Use family therapy to assist with the interactive process.
- Recognize individual family dynamics that necessitate intervention.
- As the adolescent grows older, encourage individual adolescent therapy (e.g., cognitive-behavioural, interpersonal, psychodynamic, or supportive).
- Take into account larger systemic issues.

Residential treatment and multisystem treatment are examples of interventions.

The treatment of medical illness, which addresses substance abuse when present and uses psychopharmacology to treat severe symptoms, stabilizes acute behaviour. It is illegal to prescribe medication for nonspecific, developmentally mediated disruptiveness. However, it is not illegal to prescribe medications for specific disorders (e.g., ADHD, bipolar disorder, autism), which can include disruptive behaviour as part of the core condition.

These biological interventions should be accompanied by parent management training with an adolescent focus. This type of training provides immediate strategies for behaviour control through the use of behavioural cues. Second, an assessment of the family, informed by various schools and techniques of family therapy, frequently dictates the need for intervention. Unfortunately, due to specific parental and marital dynamics, parent management interventions are frequently not implemented.

CONCLUSION:

A sizable portion of our adolescent population requires assistance in dealing with emotional and behavioural issues. Though many children from troubled families may appear normal, understanding the family context and the challenges that teenagers face helps to identify the adolescent-family dyad that requires treatment. It points to the necessity for a multifaceted approach to preventing these issues in teenagers. School-based mental health programmes can effectively address the problem by assisting victims as soon as possible. A community intervention for addiction may be necessary, and schools can serve as the focal point by implementing innovative initiatives such as student drama clubs, street plays, and other activities that educate both the family and the schoolchildren about the dangers of addiction. Although there is mounting evidence that energy drink intake is linked to detrimental social, emotional, and health effects, few studies have looked at this link in teenagers. Adolescents who consume energy drinks are at risk for a variety of harmful consequences and should be targeted for prevention. As a result, we might deduce that a loving family with marital harmony is protective against mental illness. As a parent, the most important thing you can do is accept and help your children as they are. Explain to your adolescent why they shouldn't experiment with drugs, alcohol, or sex so early in their lives. Rather than dismissing their feelings, attempt to listen and empathise with them. Encourage them to come to you if they have a problem rather than keeping it to themselves. Instead of being confrontational or violent, teach kids appropriate ways to vent frustration. Teenagers are perplexed and want direction in order to stay on the right track. They require boundaries in order to maintain control. When you make rules, you're also setting restrictions for people to follow. Teenage years are an excellent time to begin teaching decision-making abilities. Teach students how to analyse or gauge an option in a variety of ways so they can make the best decision possible.

Cognitive-behavioural therapy and skill training may be beneficial, particularly if there is comorbidity (eg, depression). While psychodynamic psychotherapy provides a framework for understanding developmental constructs, it has not been proven to be effective as a stand-alone treatment intervention. Finally, behaviourally oriented parent management training programs are perhaps the most empirically validated modality.

Working with disruptive adolescents has the ultimate goal of improving self-regulation in all domains. Although difficult, this is the foundation of child and adolescent development. Such development occurs within the family, and any treatment must support the efforts of the family who is raising children to instil the basic life skill of self-control.

REFERENCES

- Fry, P. S. (1998). The development of personal meaning and wisdom in adolescence: A reexamination of moderating and consolidating factors and influences. Lawrence Erlbaum Associates Publishers.
- Yeager, D. S., & Bundick, M. J. (2009). The role of purposeful work goals in promoting meaning in life and in schoolwork during adolescence. Journal of Adolescent Research, 24(4), 423-452.
- Pathak, R., Sharma, R. C., Parvan, U. C., Gupta, B. P., Ojha, R. K., & Goel, N. K. (2011). Behavioural and emotional problems in school going adolescents. The Australasian medical journal, 4(1), 15.
- Holubcikova, J., Kolarcik, P., Geckova, A. M., Reijneveld, S. A., & van Dijk, J. P. (2017). Regular energy drink consumption is associated with the risk of health and behavioural problems in adolescents. European journal of pediatrics, 176(5), 599-605.
- Lange, L., & Randler, C. (2011). Morningness-eveningness and behavioural problems in adolescents. Sleep and Biological Rhythms, 9(1), 12-18.
- Flouri, E., & Panourgia, C. (2014). Negative automatic thoughts and emotional and behavioural problems in adolescence. Child and Adolescent Mental Health, 19(1), 46-51.
- Derluyn, I., Broekaert, E., & Schuyten, G. (2008). Emotional and behavioural problems in migrant adolescents in Belgium. European child & adolescent psychiatry, 17(1), 54-62.

- Kantomaa, M. T., Tammelin, T. H., Demakakos, P., Ebeling, H. E., & Taanila, A. M. (2010). Physical activity, emotional and behavioural problems, maternal education and self-reported educational performance of adolescents. Health education research, 25(2), 368-379.
- Hasan, A., & Husain, A. (2016). Behavioural problems of adolescents. *IAHRW International Journal of Social Sciences*, 4(2), 238-244.
- https://www.psychiatrictimes.com/view/synthetic-cannabinoids-cathinones
- https://www.psychiatrictimes.com/view/understanding-and-managing-adolescent-disruptive-behavior

IV
A LANGUAGE DEVELOPMENT AT EARLY AGE AND ITS THEORIES

Tanwangini Sahani, Student, BBA, GGSIPU, Delhi

INTRODUCTION

Language is a method of communication that involves the use of words and the application of systematic rules to organise those words in order to communicate information from one person to another. While language is a method of communication, it is not the only one. Many species communicate with one another via postures, motions, scents, and vocalisations. For creatures that need to interact and form social ties with their conspecifics, communication is critical. The process by which children learn to interpret and communicate language in early life is known as language development. Children develop language at a quick rate from birth until they reach the age of five. Humans all go through the same phases of language development. One of the most fascinating aspects of children's language development is how closely it is linked to play. Symbolic play develops around the same time that children produce their first words, which is usually around the age of 12 to 13 months. A child placing a banana to her ear and pretending it is a phone is an example of symbolic play. It makes sense that these two processes happen at the same time in terms of development because children must first learn to think symbolically before they can use language, and language is symbolic (a word represents an object, for example). The age and rate at which a child hits each milestone of language development, on the other hand, varies substantially. As a result, rather of comparing a child's linguistic development to that of other children, one must compare it to norms. Girls learn language more quickly than boys in general. Language development reflects the brain's growth and maturation better than any other component of development. The formation of a language is a fascinating process. Learning language is, in fact, a natural process that kids are born knowing how to accomplish. Talking is a significant developmental milestone for children. By the age of 21 months, most children will be able to say 100 words, and by the age of two, they will be able to combine these words into short phrases. Unfortunately, many young children miss out on important developmental stages.

Figure 1: pinterest.com

"Late talkers" are children that have a limited expressive vocabulary (less than 40-50 words) and make no word combinations at the age of 24 months. The prevalence of language disorders, as well as their impact on literacy and reading later in life, underscores the importance of early intervention as soon as speech impairments are identified. Surprisingly, all children learn language in the same way, regardless of which language their parents speak. Language development is divided into three stages, each of which follows a predictable pattern.

Objectives

- To study different theories of language development in children
- To understand language development at first eight years
- To know what parents can do to stimulate language development

Analysis and Discussion

Figure 2: The Sri Ram Early Year

Theories of Language Development

Children learn language by imitation, according to the oldest theories on language development. While studies have indicated that toddlers who imitate the actions of others around them during their first year of life learn to speak more quickly, there is also evidence that imitation alone cannot explain how children learn to speak. There are a variety of language development theories that have been promoted by different proponents. This section looks at four major theories in depth. Behavioral theory, nativist linguistic theories, social interactionist theory, and cognitive theory are examples of these.

Behavioral Theory: Language, according to behaviourists, may be watched and quantified. Language is uttered in reaction to stimuli that trigger the need to utilise it. Competence in the rules of language is less crucial to a behaviourist than the capacity to speak it; speaking is what makes language real. Knowledge is a mental state, and a language's structure does not make it a language; it is the function of uttering words that distinguishes a language from others. B.F. Skinner is a well-known behaviourist who proposed that infants are conditioned to respond to particular stimuli with language as a result of their surroundings. Children are rewarded and grow more skilled when they speak their parents' language. They develop the ability to respond appropriately to the environmental cues provided by his parents. This has a greater impact on a child's language than understanding of rules. While most people believe that growing up in a language-rich environment helps children succeed in school, experts have yet to establish this through trials outside of the lab. The behaviourist approach has been chastised for failing to consider the various and varied factors on a child's language acquisition.

Nativist Linguistic Theories: Linguists and child psychologists have long questioned the manner in which a kid acquires language. Noam Chomsky, the founder of most nativist theories of language acquisition, drew attention to children's natural ability to learn language, which had previously been dismissed as a purely cultural process based on imitation. Children learn by their natural ability to structure the laws of language, according to nativist linguistic theories, but they cannot fully employ this gift without the presence of other humans. This does not, however, imply that the youngster requires any kind of formal instruction. According to Chomsky, children's brains are pre-programmed with a Language Acquisition Device (LAD). They are born knowing the basic concepts of language, but they must set numerous criteria (for example, whether sentences in the language(s) they are learning must have explicit subjects). According to nativist theory, when a young infant is introduced to a language, their LAD allows them to determine the parameters and deduce the grammatical rules because they are intrinsic.

- Many linguists and psychologists disagree with Chomsky's assertion, and many linguists and psychologists feel language is not as innate as Chomsky claims. Both for and against Chomsky's perspective of development, there are compelling reasons. The theory of Universal Grammar, which states that all languages have the same basic underlying structure and that specific languages have rules that turn these underlying structures into the distinctive patterns observed in given languages, is central to the Chomskian viewpoint. Another argument is that in a real human context where complete sentences are the exception, human infants would be unable to learn such complete speech patterns if they did not have a penchant for language.

- **Social Interactionist Theory**: This idea emphasises the environment and context in which a language is taught. It concentrates on language pragmatics rather than grammar, which should be addressed later. The beginning speaker and the experienced speaker—whether a kid or an adult, or a second-language learner and a fluent speaker—coexist in this technique in a negotiated relationship where feedback is always possible. The relevance of the home and cultural environment in early language acquisition is the main attraction of this strategy. Language is not an innate capacity, according to this theory. Rather, it grows out of your ability to negotiate your surroundings.
- The premise that utterances make meaning if the teacher is aware of the context is the major rationale for supporting interactionism. This is the main characteristic of the interactionist viewpoint. Thought does not create objects in this case; rather, it reflects them and the context in which they are found. The fundamental concern of early-childhood language learning is comprehension rather than grammar. Chomsky, on the other hand, believes that just absorbing words results in meaningless statements that must be remedied through the instruction of structure and grammar. One viewpoint emphasises the relationship between the learner and culture, whereas the other emphasises the relationship between the learner and the arbitrary utterances of an experienced speaker.

- **Cognitive Theory:** Jean Piaget was the one who proposed this notion. He proposed that language is composed of symbols and patterns that emerge as a child's mental powers develop. Furthermore, language is just one of several mental or cognitive tasks that humans engage in. Piaget's theories about how children's minds work and grow have had a huge impact on educational theory. His distinctive breakthrough was the significance of maturation (just growing up) in children's rising capacity to grasp their environment: they cannot perform certain activities unless they are psychologically mature enough to do so.
- His research has inspired a great deal more, much of which has weakened the specificity of his own, but his significance stems from his overarching vision, as it does from many other original scientists.

Piaget claimed that children's thinking does not grow smoothly; rather, it "takes off" at specific points and moves into whole new domains and capabilities. These shifts occurred at 18 months, 7 years, and 11 or 12 years, according to him. This has been interpreted to suggest that children before these ages are incapable of understanding things in specific ways, regardless of how intelligent they are, and has been used to plan the school curriculum.

Figure 3: playingwithwords365.com

Language Development at First Eight Years

3-12 Months: Baby will most likely coo, smile, and laugh at three months. The baby will begin to play with sounds and communicate with motions such as waving and pointing as they get older.

The baby will most likely begin babbling around the age of 4-6 months. Baby will first create single-syllable sounds like 'ba', then repeat them – 'ba ba ba'.

The 'jargon phase' follows babbling, in which the infant may appear to be saying something, but their 'speech' does not sound like words. Around the age of 12 months, children begin to speak their first words with meaning.

Talk to doctor or a child and family health nurse if kid isn't babbling or making motions by the time he or she is 12 months old.

12-18 Months: Children often say their first words with significance at this age. When a child says "Dada," for example, the child is actually addressing his father. The child's vocabulary will expand in the coming months. The child is capable of comprehending far more than they are capable of expressing. They may also follow simple commands such as "Sit down."

18 months to 2 years: The majority of children will begin to string two words together to form brief "sentences." Much of what one says will be understood by the child, and much of what the child says will be understood by one. People who are unfamiliar with the youngster will only understand around half of what the toddler says. Consult the doctor, a child and family health nurse, or another health expert if the kid does not have any words by the age of 18 months.

2-3 years: The youngster most likely speaks in three-to-four-word sentences and is improving at correctly pronouncing words. The child might be able to play and converse at the same time. By the age of three, strangers should be able to understand roughly three-quarters of what the youngster says.

3-5 years: Longer, more complicated discussions regarding the child's thoughts and feelings are likely. The youngster may also inquire about things, people, and places that are not in their immediate vicinity. 'Is it raining at Grandma's house, too?' for example. The child will most likely wish to talk about a variety of things, and their vocabulary will continue to expand. The youngster may demonstrate rudimentary grammatical awareness by employing phrases that include words like "because," "if," "so," and "when." They'll also be able to provide some fascinating stories.

5-8 years: The youngster will acquire more words and begin to understand how the sounds in language interact during the early years of school. As they learn to put words together in new ways and construct different types of sentences, the youngster will become a better storyteller. These abilities also enable the youngster to express his or her thoughts and feelings. The child will be able to hold adult-like discussions by the age of eight years.

Things Parents Can Do To Stimulate Language Development
Early years:

- Respond to the baby's vocalisations verbally.
- Speak to the infant.
- Use shared attention and sign language around the age of six months (gestures). They point to and name what they notice. When describing things, use an exaggerated voice. Make use of emotive language.
- Sing to the child from the time they are a baby until they want you to stop.
- Allow older youngsters to compose their own tunes.
- Use songs to express important information such as when it's time to go to bed, when it's time to clean up, and so on.
- Make up silly melodies or songs that express affirmations about their great attributes.

Older Toddler and Preschooler:

- Start a dialogue with the child about recent occurrences and their current activities.
- To communicate, gradually raise the complexity of syntax and language.
- Provide further information to youngsters about events, as well as what they observe and how they feel.
- To elicit their participation, read interactively. Ask inquiries, use dramatic inflections, let them predict what will happen next, point to and explain pictures, and have the youngster do the same.
- Make up stories with the youngster in which everyone contributes. This fosters not only speaking but also thinking, creation, and a sense of humour.

School Age and Beyond:

- Continue the conversation.
- Hold family gatherings.
- Gather around the table for dinner and encourage conversation. Each family member can use "Thorns & Roses" by discussing one item that went wrong and one thing that went well during the day.
- Keep gadgets at home or turned off when going out to supper.
- Discuss what happened after watching a movie or a TV show together. Encourage them to read. When they've finished a book, inquire about their feelings and thoughts.

Figure 4: child-encyclopedia.com

Recommendations and Findings

- Create vowel-like and consonant-vowel sounds like "ma," "da," and "ba" to encourage baby to make them.
- Maintain eye contact, answer with words, and imitate vocalisations with various patterns and emphasis to reinforce your efforts. To suggest a query, for example, raise voice's pitch.
- Imitate the baby's guffaws and expressions.
- Teach your child to imitate actions like clapping hands, kissing, and playing finger games like pat-a-cake, peek-a-boo, and itsy-bitsy-spider.
- Bathe, eat, and dress while conversing.
- Color recognition and item counting are both important skills to have.
- To assist express message, do motions like waving farewell.
- To link a sound with a specific meaning, use animal sounds.
- Increase vocabulary. Name body parts and explain what they are used for. "This is the shape of my nose. Flowers, brownies, popcorn, and soap are among the scents I detect."
- To demonstrate the rhythm and pattern of speech, sing basic songs or recite nursery rhymes.

- Fill a container with items familiar with. Remove the thing and have the youngster explain what it is and how to use it. "This is where I keep my ball. It bounces back to me. I have fun with it."
- Retell what happened or make up a fresh story using images of recognizable people and places.
- Encourage child to offer orders. Follow his or her instructions as he or she demonstrates how to construct a block tower.

CONCLUSION

Words aren't the only method to communicate, as any parent knows. Young children communicate with us through pointing, making eye contact, and using body language. Recognizing, supporting, and positively rewarding these language precursors pave the way for future speech and language output. However, even before they learn to point to what they want, children communicate with us in other ways. Language development is, by definition, a changing process. Exploring the many and various paths taken by language can reveal information about the evolution of more general cognitive functions. Language development research has been especially helpful in understanding the origins of function specialisation as well as the scale and flexibility of cognitive processes during learning. Children's language development is significantly influenced by the characteristics of the environment in which they grow. The rate at which a kid develops linguistic skills is determined by his or her experiences. The amount of interaction a child has with his or her parents or caregivers has a big impact on his or her language development. In addition, a child's language comprehension can be slowed by health difficulties. There are numerous ways for parents to provide opportunity for their children to develop their communication skills. Putting things just out of reach is a pleasure. Instead of delivering your son a granola bar you know he wants, place it slightly out of reach and wait for him to request it in some way.

REFERENCES

- Language Development in early childhood Essay, https://ivypanda.com/essays/language-development-in-early-childhood/, Oct 26th, 2019
- Language development, http://www.healthofchildren.com/L/Language-Development.html
- Language development in children: what you need to know, https://raisingchildren.net.au/babies/development/language-

development/language-development-0-8

- Language Development, https://courses.lumenlearning.com/wmopen-psychology/chapter/language/
- How Do Children Learn Language?, https://www.verywellfamily.com/how-do-children-learn-language-1449116, Carol Bainbridge, March 23, 2021
- Language Development In Children, https://childdevelopmentinfo.com/child-development/language_development/#gs.3w8u01 | Child Development InstituteLanguage Development
- Language development, https://www.sciencedirect.com/topics/agricultural-and-biological-sciences/language-development, Neurology and Clinical Neuroscience, 2007
- Language Development in Children, https://www.news-medical.net/health/Language-Development-in-Children.aspx, Sally Robertson
- Theories of Language Development in Children, https://www.kenpro.org/papers/theories-of-language-development-in-children.htm, Anthony M. Wanjohi
- How can you encourage a child's language development?, https://www.nct.org.uk/baby-toddler/learning-talk-and-communication-your-baby/how-can-you-encourage-childs-language-development
- Activities to Encourage Speech and Language Development, https://www.readingrockets.org/article/activities-encourage-speech-and-language-development, American Speech-Language-Hearing Association

V
COGNITIVE AND MORAL DEVELOPMENT IN LEARNERS

Mr. K. C. Malik, Associate Professor, Sri Venkateswara College, University of Delhi.
Divine Tomar, Pupil Teacher, Manvi Institute of Education And Technology, Scert,

INTRODUCTION

COGNITIVE DEVELOPMENT

Cognitive development means how children think, explore and figure things out. It is the growth of information, skills, problem-solving abilities, and attitudes that enable children to think about and comprehend the world around them. Cognitive development includes brain development. Attention, short-term memory, long-term memory, logic & reasoning, auditory processing, visual processing, and processing speed are all cognitive capabilities. They are the abilities that the brain employs to think, learn, read, remember, focus, and solve issues.

Source: www.lumenlearning.com

Children gather, sort, and analyse data from their environment, which they then use to improve their perceptual and thinking skills. Early in life, the essential character of intelligence is established, and development entails the accumulation of increasingly more learning experiences.

VIEWS OF PIAGET, BRUNER AND VYGOTSKY ON COGNITIVE DEVELOPMENT

JEAN PIAGET

Source: www.thefamouspeople.com

During the twentieth century, Jean Piaget (1896-1980) was one of the most influential researchers in the field of developmental psychology. Piaget was educated in biology and philosophy and referred to himself as a "genetic epistemologist." He was particularly interested in biological influences on "how we learn." He claimed that our ability to undertake "abstract symbolic reasoning" is what sets us apart from other animals. Piaget's ideas are frequently contrasted with those of Lev Vygotsky (1896-1934), who saw social interaction as the major wellspring of cognition and behaviour. Piaget became interested in how children think while working at Binet's IQ test facility in Paris. He saw that young children's replies were qualitatively different from older children's, implying that the younger ones were not stupid than their older friends, but rather answered the questions differently because they thought differently. The importance of Piaget's ideas on child psychology today can be summarised by his views on education and teacher training. Although Jean Piaget's theory of cognitive development is well-known, most sociologists are unfamiliar with his name. Although Piaget was primarily interested in individual development, he felt that child-to-child interaction plays a role in cognitive development. Since the last formulations of Piaget's constructivism four decades ago, cognitive developmental psychology has undergone profound alterations. Theories of cognitive development have sparked long and bitter debates that have been heavy on rhetoric but light on facts. Piagetian views of cognitive development as arising from self-directed behaviour throughout infancy are the foundations of constructivist theory. Because Piaget's views on childhood were so well-known and accepted, at least one component of development seemed certain to many psychologists: human infants went through a long time in which they are unable to reason. They can learn to recognise items and grin at them, as well as crawl and control objects, but they lack conceptions and ideas. This time, which Piaget dubbed the sensorimotor stage of development, was thought to last until a child was one-and-a-half to two years old. Infants learn how to represent the world in a symbolic, conceptual man? Ner near the end of this stage, and thus progress from infancy to early childhood. According to Jean Piaget's theory of cognitive development, children's intellect evolves through time. A kid's cognitive growth entails more than just collecting information; the youngster must also create or develop a mental picture of the world. Piaget stressed universal cognitive change as a result.

JEROME SEYMOUR BRUNER

Source: www.washingtonpost.com

Bruner, Jerome Seymour, was an American psychologist who made significant contributions to human cognitive psychology and educational psychology's cognitive learning theory. Jerome Bruner, a psychologist by training, has always been and continues to be one of the most influential individuals in education. In the 1960s and 1970s, his educational philosophy had a direct impact on the educational programmes that were developed throughout those decades. Bruner believes that learners develop their own knowledge by employing a coding system to organise and categorise information. Bruner believed that discovering a coding system rather than being informed by a teacher is the most efficient approach to do so. Jerome Bruner was a key figure in the Cognitive Revolution, which brought behaviourism to an end in American psychology and put cognition at the forefront. Bruner argues for the primacy of 'meaning-making' in human action in his reassessment of the cognitive revolution, saying that toddlers learn to give meaning to what individuals do as they learn the language and social practices of their culture. The importance of attribution of mental states to others has been examined extensively in a new research area known as children's "theory of mind" over the last decade.

Unlike Bruner, who views psychology as a natural empirical science, researchers in this discipline consider the child as developing a causal theory to explain and predict human behaviour.

LEV SEMYONOVICH VYGOTSKY

Source: www.curriculumsolutions.com

Lev Semyonovich Vygotsky was a Soviet psychologist who specialised in child psychological development. Over the last several decades, Lev Vygotsky's (1934) work has served as the foundation for much research and theory in cognitive development, notably what has come to be known as sociocultural theory. Human development is viewed as a socially mediated process in which children acquire cultural values, beliefs, and problem-solving skills through collaborative conversations with more informed members of society, according to Vygotsky's sociocultural theory. Culture-specific tools, private speech, and the Zone of Proximal Development are all notions in Vygotsky's theory. Vygotsky's theories emphasise the importance of social contact in the formation of cognition (Vygotsky, 1978), since he strongly believed that community plays an important role in the process of "creating meaning."

Unlike Piaget, who believed that children's growth must come first, Vygotsky believed that "learning is an essential and universal part of the process of establishing culturally organised, specifically human psychological function." Vygotsky pioneered a sociocultural perspective on cognitive development. He formed his theories at roughly the same time that Jean Piaget was starting to develop his ideas (1920's and 30's), but he died at the age of 38, and so his theories remain incomplete – although some of his publications are currently being translated from Russian. Vygotsky emphasises the role of culture in cognitive development. Vygotsky believes that cognitive development differs by culture. Vygotsky lays a greater emphasis on the social aspects that influence cognitive development. For learning, Vygotsky emphasises the importance of cultural and social context. Children and their partners co-construct knowledge as a result of social interactions from guided learning within the zone of proximal development. Vygotsky emphasises the function of language in cognitive development more (and in a different way) than others. Cognitive development, according to Vygotsky, is the product of linguistic internalisation. Adults, according to Vygotsky, are a crucial source of cognitive development. Vygotsky stated that children are born with "elementary mental functions," which he defined as "fundamental skills for intellectual development." Vygotsky, like Piaget, believes that young children are naturally curious and actively involved in their own learning, as well as the discovery and development of new knowledge.

MORAL DEVELOPMENT

The psychology study of moral growth has grown significantly, both in terms of theoretical diversity and in terms of the number of theoretical viewpoints represented in the area. Children form configurations of thinking about welfare, justice, and rights linked to feelings like attachment, sympathy, and empathy, according to a structural developmental relational perspective. Children form systems of judgements in the domains of social convention, which include uniformities within social systems, and the personal domain, which involves understandings of permissible realms of choice, freedoms, and autonomy, in addition to moral judgments. Moral, conventional, and personal judgments are unique from one another in this social domain approach, and they form separate growth trajectories. Adulthood phases for moral growth are discussed after evaluating the qualities of the cognitive-developmental stage concept, which has previously been limited in its application to child and adolescent development. Other approaches to moral formation and accompanying basic psychological assumptions are compared to the structural relational domain approach. From birth through adulthood, moral development is concerned with the emergence, change, and comprehension of morality.

Morality develops during the course of a person's life and is influenced by their experiences and conduct when confronted with moral concerns at various stages of physical and cognitive development. In summary, morality is concerned with an individual's developing sense of what is good and wrong; as a result, young children's moral judgement and character differ from that of an adult. Morality is frequently used interchangeably with the terms "rightness" and "goodness." It refers to a code of conduct that guides one's activities, behaviours, and beliefs and is drawn from one's culture, religion, or personal philosophy.

LAWRENCE KOHLBERG

educationaltechnology.net

Lawrence Kohlberg was an American psychologist who is best known for his moral development phases theory. He devised a research programme to better understand moral development–which he referred to as justice development–over the course of a lifetime. Kohlberg investigated the stage of development and moral perspectives of children, adolescents, and adults in the United States and overseas using dilemma interviews and a detailed scoring manual. He talked about the relationship between judgement and action, the transnational universality of moral development, and gender-related morality in this context. His groundbreaking interdisciplinary work spanned subjects as diverse as developmental psychology, philosophy, and education, to name a few. His study was inspirational in many ways and will continue to be inspirational for years to come. Lawrence Kohlberg has been advancing his cognitive development hypothesis of moralization, which has become prominent in the study of moral development and its application to moral education, for nearly three decades. Kohlberg's moral development theory is concerned with how children learn morality and moral reasoning. According to Kohlberg's thesis, moral development develops in six stages.

The theory also suggests that moral logic is primarily focused on seeking and maintaining justice. Each stage offers a new perspective, but not everyone functions at the highest level all the time. There were three levels of moral reasoning that encompassed the six stages. The three levels were **Pre-Conventional, Conventional and post conventional. The six stages are:**

Stage 1: The first stage emphasizes children's self-interest in decision-making as they try to avoid punishment at all costs. Kohlberg considers children's moral thinking. They believe that regulations are expected to be observed at a young age, and that people in control will definitely punish them.

Stage 2: This stage examines how youngsters learn to embrace the viewpoints taught, while simultaneously acknowledging that there are several points of view on each topic. Each person is unique and, as a result, will have a distinct perspective based on their interests.

Stage 3: This stage acknowledges the desire to be accepted into societal groupings, as well as how the outcome affects each individual.

Stage 4: Laws and social order are supreme at this point. It is necessary to follow and obey the rules and regulations. Stage four depicts a person's moral growth as a member of a larger society. Everyone becomes more conscious of how their activities affect others and concentrates on their own position, following rules, and respecting authorities.

Stage 5: This stage acknowledges the introduction of abstract reasoning as people attempt to explain specific behaviors.

Stage 6: Moral reasoning is founded on personal values, according to the final step of Kohlberg's theory. When Kohlberg recognised that elected methods do not always provide fair outcomes, he created Stage 6. To acknowledge the application of justice in moral thinking, the sixth stage was formed. As a starting point for what is good and just, general, universal morality and ethics are applied. These are frequently abstract concepts that can only be sketched rather than defined. Universal principles are based on values like equality, fairness, dignity, and respect.

CONCLUSION

According to Kohlberg's findings, each stage of moral development occurs one at a time and in the same order. Moral growth is invariant; individuals progress through the phases one at a time and in a predetermined order, but some may never reach the ultimate level. He also came to the conclusion that the stages' order is universal across all cultures.

REFERENCES

Tudge, J., & Rogoff, B. (1999). Peer influences on cognitive development: Piagetian and Vygotskian perspectives. Lev Vygotsky: critical assessments, 3, 32-56.

Mandler, J. M. (1990). A new perspective on cognitive development in infancy. American Scientist, 78(3), 236-243.

Takaya, K. (2008). Jerome Bruner's theory of education: From early Bruner to later Bruner. Interchange, 39(1), 1-19.

Astington, J. W., & Olson, D. R. (1995). The cognitive revolution in children's understanding of mind. Human development, 38(4-5), 179-189.

Huitt, W., & Hummel, J. (2003). Piaget's theory of cognitive development. Educational psychology interactive, 3(2), 1-5.

McLeod, S. A. (2014). Lev vygotsky.

Piaget, J. (1965). The moral development. New York: Free Press, 1(1), 0.

Turiel, E. (2015). Moral development. Handbook of child psychology and developmental science, 1-39.

Kohlberg, L. (1986). Lawrence Kohlberg, consensus and controversy (No. 1). Routledge.

VI
PERSONALITY CONCEPTS AND THEORIES

Swati singh, Student, Guru Nanak Dev. Institute of Technology, Delhi.
B.Voc. Software Development

INTRODUCTION

Personality Concept

Personality refers to a person's mental and physical well-being.

Davidson*writes on temperament, that is socially developed once having a genetic base, through time in his medical textbook, "Principles and observe of drugs." once passing through a succession of biological process stages, the individual reaches associate adult psychological stage.*

*"Personality is that the most applicable conceptualization of a person's behaviour with all its characteristics, that the soul will offer in an exceedingly moment," **McClelland says.***

***According to Davidson's** conception, there area unit three completely different parts of one's temperament and its development and growth: social, physiological, and psychological.*

***McClelland** has targeted on the psychological factors that influence desired changes in {an individual's|a person's|a temperament's|a human|somebody's} behaviour and personality.*

As a result, each of those ideas shed some light-weight on the formation of temperament and individual behaviour. Excluding **Allport's** comprehensive approach to the topic, each of those definitions have the foremost application and utility in organisational behaviour.

An individual's temperament is exclusive, personal, and a primary issue of his behaviour.

Individuals answer completely different events in several ways that thanks to variances in temperament. Some temperament theorists highlight the necessity of recognising the person-situation interaction, i.e., personality's social learning parts. The study of human behaviour would profit greatly from such associate interpretation.

Source:Corporate Finance institute

Personality Nature

Every person's temperament is expounded to his or her nature. In general, someone asserts himself by his temperament traits. With their years of expertise, mature folks adopt associate objective perspective toward themselves et al.. They conjointly mirror on themselves so as to reinforce their temperament and behavior.

i. Self-Consciousness:

People at large and alternative species area unit immensely completely different. His temperament is marked by a attribute notable as 'self-consciousness,' that permits him to remember of his surroundings and self-identity.

ii. Atmosphere Adaptability:

Off and on, temperament will build diversifications in response to desired changes. The term "resistance to change" refers to a disagreement defined by tension and conflict. folks sometimes comply with new surroundings and obstacles. Adaptation to new settings is usually in the middle of a modification in behaviour pattern, leading to a sleek operating condition and a nice atmosphere.

iii. Goal-oriented:

Folks try and accomplish their objectives. people do have the motivation to realize their objectives. Motive is that the results of needs and necessities. a person's want leads his or her behaviour toward achieving that want. activity changes area unit influenced by each physiological and social factors.

iv. Temperament Integration:

temperament works in an exceedingly consistent manner by combining varied activities (both mental and private experiences). temperament comes in an exceedingly kind of shapes and sizes. Temperament is differentiated by the style within which it's integrated. Folks with developed personalities have a powerful association to their values and experiences. This can be determined by their activity standards that they need developed from childhood.

Personality characteristics

You'll be asked to list your personal attributes if you apply for employment. Employers assume that your temperament is much fastened and will not vary considerably from year to year. Whereas most folks will relate to the current notion, wherever will our temperament originate? Is it in our polymer, or is it additional a results of our formative circumstances?

The answer is, of course, both. As a result of our brain and therefore the chemicals that act inside it area unit generated by genes, there area unit bound to be genes that influence our behaviour. Finding anybody of the many genes concerned, on the opposite hand, is notoriously tough. as a result of personalities area unit complicated, the biology of behaviour is as complicated.

Scientist's area unit solely currently commencing to gain a more robust understanding of however genes have an effect on behaviour.

i. Temperament is well-structured and consistent.

ii. Temperament may be a psychological attribute that's influenced by biological processes and necessities.

iii. Temperament influences however folks behave.

iv. Temperament is expressed in an exceedingly kind of ways that, together with thoughts, feelings, and behaviours.

Who Were the Neo-Freudians?

Many of the most tenets of Freud's psychotherapy theory were given by Neo-Freudian psychologists, however they updated and tailored the approach to accommodate their own beliefs, thoughts, and opinions. Scientist brain doctor instructed a spread of polemic views, however he conjointly no inheritable an oversized following.

Many of those students united with Freud's ideas regarding the unconscious and therefore the importance of childhood development. Alternative students, on the opposite hand, disagreed or outright rejected variety of things. As a result, these people developed their own distinct conceptions of temperament and psychological feature.

Neo-Freudian Disagreements

These neo-Freudian thinkers disagreed with neurologist for a spread of reasons. Erik Erikson, as an example, argued that brain doctor was mistaken in basic cognitive process that childhood events affected temperament virtually entirely. Alternative considerations that role player neo-Freudian philosophers' attention were:

The importance of sexual needs as a basic motive in Freud's theory

The absence of social and cultural influences on behaviour and temperament in Freud's work

Sigmund Freud's demoralised read on attribute

Many neo-Freudians believed that Freud's theories were too targeted on psychopathology, sex, and childhood events.

Instead, several of them selected to focus their theories on a lot of positive aspects of attribute moreover because the social influences that contribute to temperament and behavior.1

While the neo-Freudians might are influenced by Freud, they developed their own distinctive theories and views on human development, temperament, and behavior.

Major Neo-Freudian Thinkers

There were variety of neo-Freudian thinkers World Health Organization stone-broke with the brain doctor psychotherapy tradition to develop their own psychodynamic theories. a number of these people were at first a part of Freud's set, as well as Carl Jung and male monarch Adler.

Carl Jung

Carl Jung and Freud once had an in depth relationship, however Carl Gustav Jung stone-broke away to make his own concepts.2 Carl Gustav Jung observed his theory of temperament as analytical scientific discipline, and he introduced the conception of the collective unconscious. He delineated this as a universal structure shared by all members of an equivalent species containing all of the instincts and archetypes that influence human behavior.

Jung still placed nice stress on the unconscious, however his theory placed a better stress on his conception of the collective unconscious instead of the private unconscious. Like several of the opposite neo-Freudians, Carl Gustav Jung conjointly centered less on sex than Freud did in his work.

Alfred Adler

Alfred Adler believed that Freud's theories centered too heavily on sex because the primary incentive for human behavior.Instead, Adler placed a lesser stress on the role of the unconscious and a larger target social and social influences.

His approach, called individual scientific discipline, was focused on the drive that each one folks need to complete their feelings of inferiority. The complex, he urged, was somebody's feelings and doubts that they are doing not qualify to people or to society's expectations.4

Erik Erikson

While Freud believed that temperament was largely set in stone throughout time of life, Erikson felt that development continuing throughout life. He conjointly believed that not all conflicts were unconscious. He thought several were aware and resulted from the method|biological process} process itself.

Erikson de-emphasized the role of sex as a incentive for behavior and instead placed a far stronger target the role of social relationships.

His eight-stage theory of psychosocial development concentrates on a series of biological process conflicts that occur throughout the period of time, from birth till death. At every stage, folks face a crisis that has got to be resolved to develop sure psychological strengths.5

Karen Horney

Karen Horney was one amongst the primary girls trained in psychotherapy, and she or he was conjointly one amongst the primary to criticize Freud's depictions of ladies as inferior to men. Horney objected to

Freud's portrayal of ladies as full of "penis envy."

Instead, she steered that men expertise "womb envy" as a result of they're unable involved youngsters. Her theory focuses on however behavior was influenced by variety of various neurotic desires.

Trait Theories of Personalities

Trait theorists believe temperament are often understood by positing that every one individuals have sure traits, or characteristic ways in which of behaving. does one tend to be sociable or shy? Passive or aggressive? Optimistic or pessimistic? in keeping with the Diagnostic and applied mathematics Manual (DSM) of the yank medicine Association, temperament traits ar outstanding aspects of temperament that ar exhibited in an exceedingly wide selection of necessary social and private contexts. In alternative words, people have sure characteristics that partially confirm their behavior; these traits ar trends in behavior or angle that tend to be gift in spite of matters.

An example of a attribute is extraversion–introversion. sociableness tends to be manifested in outgoing, talkative, energetic behavior, whereas introversion is manifested in additional reserved and solitary behavior. a personal might fall on any purpose within the time, and therefore the location wherever the individual falls can confirm however he or she responds to varied things.

The idea of categorizing individuals by traits are often derived back as so much as Hippocrates; but additional fashionable theories have come back from Gordon Allport, Raymond Cattell, and Hans Eysenck.

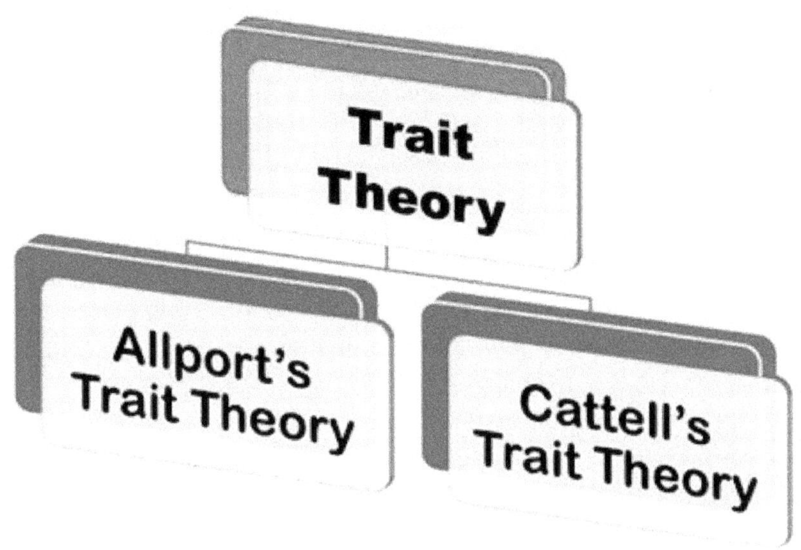

Source:Business Jargons

Gordon Allport (1897–1967)

Gordon Allport was one amongst the primary fashionable attribute theorists. Allport and Henry Odbert worked through 2 of the foremost comprehensive dictionaries of English language on the market and extracted around eighteen,000 personality-describing words. From this list they reduced the amount of words to roughly four,500 temperament-describing adjectives that they thought of to explain noticeable and comparatively permanent personality traits.

Allport organized these traits into a hierarchy of 3 levels:

Cardinal traits dominate Associate in Nursingd form an individual's behavior, like Ebenezer Scrooge's greed or Mother Theresa's unselfishness. They stand at the highest of the hierarchy and ar jointly referred to as the individual's master management. they're thought of to be Associate in Nursing individual's ruling passions. Cardinal traits ar powerful, however few individuals have personalities dominated by one attribute. Instead, our personalities ar generally composed of multiple traits.

Central traits come back next within the hierarchy. These ar general characteristics found in variable degrees in all and sundry (such as loyalty, kindness, agreeableness, friendliness, sneakiness, wildness, or grouchiness). They're the essential building blocks that form most of our behavior.

Secondary traits exist at all-time low of the hierarchy and don't seem to be quite as obvious or consistent as central traits. {they ar|they're} plentiful however are solely gift below specific circumstances; they embody things like preferences and attitudes. These secondary traits justify why someone might sometimes exhibit behaviors that appear incongruent with their usual behaviors. As an example, a friendly person gets Associate in Nursinggry once individuals attempt to tickle him; another isn't an anxious person however continuously nervous speaking in public feels.

Allport hypothesized that internal Associate in Nursing external forces influence an individual's behavior and temperament, and he stated these forces as genotypes and phenotypes. Genotypes ar internal forces that relate to however someone retains data and uses it to act with the globe. Phenotypes ar external forces that relate to the approach a personal accepts his or her surroundings and the way others influence his or her behavior.

Raymond Cattell (1905–1998)

In a trial to create Allport's list of four, 500 traits additional manageable, Raymond Cattell took the list and removed all the synonyms, reducing the amount right down to 171. However, speech communication that a attribute is either gift or absent doesn't accurately replicate a person's individuation, as a result of (according to attribute theorists) all of our personalities are literally created from constant attributes; we have a tendency to take issue solely within the degree to that every trait is expressed.

Cattell believed it necessary to sample a large vary of variables to capture a full understanding of temperament. The primary kind of knowledge was life knowledge that involves aggregation data from Associate in nursing individual's natural existence behaviors. Experimental knowledge involves activity reactions to standardized experimental things, and form knowledge involves gathering responses supported thoughtfulness by a personal concerning his or her own behavior and feelings. exploitation this knowledge, Cattell performed correlational analysis to generated sixteen dimensions of human temperament traits: preoccupancy, warmth, apprehension, emotional stability, liveliness, openness to alter, disposition, privateness, intelligence , rule consciousness , tension, sensitivity, social boldness, independence, vigilance, and dominance.

Based on these sixteen factors, he developed a questionnaire referred to as the 16PF. rather than a attribute being gift or absent, every dimension is scored over a time, from high to low. as an example, your level heatth|of heat] describes however warm, caring, and nice to others you're. If you score low on this index, you tend to be additional distant and cold. A high score on this index signifies you're corroboratory and comforting. Despite reducing considerably on Allport's list of traits, Cattell's 16PF theory has still been criticized for being too broad.

Hans Eysenck (1916–1997)

Hans Eysenck was a temperament theorizer World Health Organization targeted on temperament—innate, genetically primarily based temperament variations. He believed temperament is essentially ruled by biology, and he viewed individuals as having 2 specific temperament dimensions: sociableness vs. introversion and psychological disorder vs. stability. Once collaborating together with his married woman and fellow temperament theorizer Sybil H. J. Eysenck, he supplementary a 3rd dimension to the present model: psychoticism vs. socialization.

According to their theory, individuals high on the attribute of sociableness area unit sociable and outgoing and without delay connect with others, whereas individuals high on the attribute of introversion have the next have to be compelled to be alone, interact in solitary behaviors, and limit their interactions with others.

In the neuroticism/stability dimension, individuals high on psychological disorder tend to be associate degreexious; they have a tendency to possess an active sympathetic systema nervosum and even with low stress, their bodies and spirit tend to travel into a flight-or-fight reaction. In distinction, individuals high on stability tend to want additional stimulation to activate their flight-or-fight reaction and area unit so thought-about additional showing emotion stable.

CONCLUSION

The study of the theories of temperament is vital for college students because it prompts the requirement tounderstand why individuals behave as they are doing. Also, this space of study enlightens individuals on the requirement to be a lot of kind once judgement others supported however they behave since it's going to not be as a results of their own selection. The theories of privateity ar numerous relating to the character of personal behavior descriptions. additionally to the common theories, a reasonably uncommon conception, epigenetics is highlighted within the study of temperament theories. The range of personalities and therefore the relationships between the theories describing them points to the very fact that the human observation done by the theorists was correct to an oversized extent.

REFERENCES

- https://www.economicsdiscussion.net/management/personality/personality-introduction/32465
- https://www.verywellmind.com/who-were-the-neo-freudians-2795576
- https://courses.lumenlearning.com/boundless-psychology/chapter/trait-perspectives-on-personality/
- https://www.coursehero.com/file/p4t8mfk/Conclusion-The-study-of-the-theories-of-personality-is-important-for-students/#:~:text=described%20my%20personality.-,Conclusion%20The%20study%20of%20the%20t
- https://www.britannica.com/topic/personality
- https://www.verywellmind.com/what-is-personality-2795416
- https://courses.lumenlearning.com/boundless-psychology/chapter/introduction-to-personality/
- https://www.apa.org/topics/personality

VII
UNDERSTANDING THE DEVELOPMENTAL CHARACTERISTICS OF THE LEARNER

Dr. Ekata Gupta, Associate Professor, Guru Nanak Institute of management, Delhi

Pranati Das, Student-, BBA, Meerabai Institute of Technology

INTRODUCTION

Concept of Development

The Learning Objective's Concept is the overarching notion or generalization. You directly teach the concept, what it is, the generalization, and the major idea to the pupils in Concept Development. A documented, ironclad definition, as well as examples and non-examples, are included in the Concept (if applicable). The Learning Objective should be the source of the Concept. In the Learning Objective, it is frequently the noun:

Example:

- Make inferences based on the information provided in the text.
- Calculate a rectangular prism's volume.
- Describe the mitotic process.
- Describe the United States Constitution's checks and balances.

Although most concepts are nouns, some, like Add numbers to 10 using objects, can be verbs. In this situation, the concept or main idea is that adding means figuring out how much you have in total.

What is Included in Concept Development?

A bulletproof definition or rule containing the concept's important qualities must be included in the Concept. Exercising the concept by disclosing essential, non-critical, and shared attributes, examples and non-examples (if applicable) are offered. To emphasise those qualities, examples are presented. Non-examples aid in the clarification of the idea or demonstrate how some of the concept's characteristics are frequently shared with other concepts.

A concept has properties that are critical, non-critical, and shared.

- The presence of critical qualities is unavoidable.
- At times, non-critical properties are present. To provide clarity or further information about a concept, additional statements or phrases may be required.
- Other notions can share similar properties. To prevent pupils from overgeneralizing, it's critical to demonstrate them how qualities are related to other concepts.

Why is Concept Development Relevant?

The importance of concept development can be summed up as follows:

1. Concept development is crucial since it requires the instructor to have a clear understanding and explanation of what is being taught, as well as a written reference for students, particularly English Learners.
2. Students need to develop concepts so that they can generalise new situations in school and in real life. Students require a strong conceptual foundation before they can apply what they've learned to new situations. Students, for example, can calculate how much paint is needed to paint a wall since they realise that determining area is involved.
3. Concept development is necessary so that students can internalise the generalisation rather than learning specific examples. Teach the rule that Days of the Week are usually capitalised, for example. Instead of teaching pupils about individual days, this is a generic guideline that they may apply to any day of the week. According to brain studies (Allard 2007), in order for knowledge to be kept in long-term memory, it should

be delivered in generalizations (one hook) rather than specific examples (many random hooks). Students' information is not stored in long-term memory if they are not taught concepts.

4. Because all students should be able to express the topics being taught, concept development is important. According to Richard Clark, Paul Kirschner, and John Sweller's paper Putting Children on the Path of Learning, students with no relevant concepts in long-term memory will hunt for solutions blindly for long periods of time and learn absolutely nothing.

5. State examinations and Common Core Assessments are used to assess concepts. The notion primary idea in the question is used in the 5th grade Smarter Balanced Assessment, for example. In order to select the proper answer, students will need to understand what the key idea is.

Principles of Growth & Development and their Educational Implication

Introduction: -

Concepts are assessed through state exams and Common Core Assessments. The principal idea of the question, for example, is used in the 5th grade Smarter Balanced Assessment. Students will need to understand the essential notion in order to choose the correct answer.

Meaning of Growth: -

State tests and Common Core Assessments are used to evaluate concepts. In the 5th grade Smarter Balanced Assessment, for example, the question's main premise is employed. In order to choose the proper answer, students must first grasp the fundamental concept.

Definition: -

Arnold Gessel claims that "Rather than the environment, growth is a function of the organism. The environment provides the soil and surroundings for development manifestations, but these manifestations are the result of an inherent, inner organism and an intrinsic development physiology. Growth is such a complex and delicate process that it necessitates strong stabilising mechanisms, as well as an inherent balance in the overall pattern and direction of the growth trend."

Meaning of Development: -

Overall changes in shape, form, or structure are referred to as development. Development is a lifelong and ongoing process. It begins with the birth of a kid and concludes with the individual's death. The term "development" refers to the changes that occur in an organism as a whole, rather than the changes that occur in individual sections.

Definition: -

Development psychology is concerned with the study of behavioural changes across time. It refers to a process in which a person's growth and capabilities vary throughout time as a result of maturation and interaction with the environment.

Principles of Growth and Development: -

· **Principle of community:**

Community development is a result of community development. It never stops from the womb to the tomb. Every person develops his or her body and mind from the moment he or she is born.

· **Principle of Individual differences:**

Individual variations in development are unaffected. Each youngster develops at his or her own pace.

· **Principle of orderly development:**

The process of development progresses from broad to specific. The youngster first learns general information before moving on to detailed or specific information.

· **Uniformity of pattern:**

Although development does not occur at the same rate for everyone and differs significantly from one person to the next, it does follow a predictable pattern.

· **Principle of interaction and maturation and learning:**

Maturation and learning both contribute to growth and development. Maturation refers to changes in a developing organism, whereas learning refers to behavioural changes.

- **Principle of unique development:**

Individuals differ in terms of their time patterns, e.g., all children start sitting up, crawling, and standing up at the same time.

- **Principle of differential development:**

There is a principle that male and female children develop differently. In comparison to boys, girls mature earlier.

- **Principle of inter- related development:**

The process of development is holistic. His physical, intellectual, emotional, social, and other types of growth are all intertwined and dependent on one another.

Educational Implication

For parents, instructors, and educators, understanding the principles of growth and development is extremely important and beneficial. The following are some examples of how growth and development principles might be applied: -

- **Adjusting school program: -**

It assists the instructor in adapting the school programme, procedures, and practices to the child's level of development, allowing him to become more productive in the classroom.

- **Sympathetic Handling: -**

It assists parents and teachers in treating their children or students sympathetically and realistically solving their difficulties.

- **Effective guidance: -**

It assists the instructor in treating the right guidance programme by allowing the teacher to grasp the individual differences of the pupils.

- **Importance of childhood period: -**

It assists parents and teachers in comprehending the significance of the childhood era. As a result, parents and instructors should provide a wide range of social and emotional experiences for their children.

- **Right expectation: -**

Its knowledge enables us to anticipate what to expect from an individual child in terms of physical, mental, and social development at various phases of development.

- **Importance of environment: -**

It aids parents and teachers in understanding and instilling the value of heredity and a healthy environment, as well as assisting us in paying proper attention to environmental conditions.

Characteristics of Development

The following are some of the most essential development characteristics:

- **Development as a continuous process: -**

The process of growth and development begins at conception and continues until the individual reaches' adulthood. It progresses at a steady but steady pace rather than in leaps and bounds. Both physical and mental features develop progressively until they achieve their ultimate potential.

- **Development proceeds from general to specific response: -**

To begin with, a child's response or reactions are of a generic type. He uses his entire body to react to the circumstance and external inputs. He gradually develops distinct answers. This is true not only of his bodily responses, but also of his cognitive and emotional responses. A child's reactions, which are initially general in character, later become more specific. This is an indication of maturation and growth.

- **Development follows a pattern: -**

Development takes place in a systematic and sequential manner. Thus, the sequence of human development is infancy, early childhood, later childhood, adolescence, and adulthood.

- **Different aspect of growth develops at different stages: -**

Despite the fact that development is a continual process, the rate of growth is not consistent. As a result, there are times of rapid growth and periods of slow growth. The pace of growth slows throughout the first three years of life, but accelerates again during the adolescent stage. Similarly, not all areas of the body grow at the same rate, and not all aspects of mental development evolve at the same rate. As a result, they mature at various times.

- **Most traits are correlated in development: -**

In general, it has been assumed that a child with above-average intellectual development is also exceptional in many other areas, such as health, sociability, and unique aptitudes. Similarly, his mental development is intertwined with his physical development.

- **Development is a product of interaction of the organism and environment: -**

Neither genes nor the environment alone is responsible for an individual's development. Both are responsible for human growth and development, while it is impossible to say exactly how much genetics and environment play a role in an individual's development.

- **Growth is both quantitative and qualitative: -**

As a child develops physically, he also develops qualitatively in terms of his personality. That is to say, when a youngster grows older, his mental and emotional functions develop as well. As a result, these two qualities are inextricably linked.

Cognitive development

Cognitive development is the process through which a person perceives, thinks about, and comprehends his or her environment as a result of the interaction of hereditary and learned elements. Information processing, intelligence, reasoning, language development, and memory are all components of cognitive development.

It was long thought that infants lacked the ability to comprehend or develop complex concepts, and that they would stay cognitively deficient until they learnt to speak. From the moment they are born, newborns are aware of their surroundings and interested in exploring them. Babies begin to actively learn from the moment they are born. They gather, sort, and interpret data from everywhere around them, then use it to improve their perceptual and reasoning abilities.

Piaget's theory of development: -

The theory of cognitive development developed by French scientist Jean Piaget (1896–1980) is the most well-known and influential. Piaget's hypothesis, initially published in 1952, was based on decades of detailed observation of children in their natural circumstances, including his own, as opposed to behaviorists' laboratory trials. Piaget was concerned in how children reacted to their surroundings, but he proposed a more active role for them than learning theory predicted. He saw a child's knowledge as being made up of schemas, which he defined as "fundamental units of knowledge used to organize past experiences and provide a foundation for understanding future ones."

Assimilation and accommodation, two complimentary processes identified by Piaget, are constantly changing schemas. Assimilation is the process of assimilating new data by incorporating it into an existing schema. To put it another way, humans assimilate new experiences by linking them to previous experiences. Accommodation, on the other hand, occurs when the schema itself changes to accommodate new information. Piaget defined cognitive development as a constant effort to achieve equilibration, which he defined as a balance between assimilation and accommodation.

Infancy: -

Infants learn to utilize their senses to investigate the world around them as soon as they are born. Most babies can focus on and follow moving objects, recognize pitch and loudness of sound, see all colors and discern hue and brightness, and begin anticipating events such as sucking at the sight of a nipple. Infants can remember faces, reproduce facial emotions such as smiling and frowning, and respond to familiar sounds by the age of three months.

Babies are just six months old when they begin to comprehend how the world works. They copy sounds, like hearing their own voice, recognize their parents, avoid strangers, distinguish between animate and inanimate objects, and measure distance based on object size. They also understand that if they drop an object, they can retrieve it. Babies can recognize their names between the ages of four and seven months.

Toddlerhood: -

Toddlers have achieved the "sensorimotor" stage of Piaget's theory of cognitive development, which involves rudimentary reasoning, between the ages of 18 months and three years. For example, they can recognize the permanence of items and people, follow the displacement of objects visually, and use instruments and equipment. Toddlers begin to seek greater independence, which can provide difficulties for parents concerned about their children's safety. They also comprehend discipline and what constitutes appropriate and inappropriate behavior, as well as the meanings of phrases such as "please" and "thank you."

Preschool: -

Preschoolers, ages three to six, should be in Piaget's cognitive development theory's "preoperational" stage, which means they are using their imagery and memory skills. They should be taught to study and memories, and their worldview is typically quite self-centered. Preschoolers have often developed social interaction abilities, such as playing and cooperating with other kids their age. It's typical for preschoolers to push their cognitive capacities to their limits, and they pick up on bad concepts and behaviors like talking back to adults, lying, and bullying. Preschoolers' cognitive development also includes increasing their attention span, learning to read, and forming disciplined routines, such as doing housework.

School age: -

Younger school-age children, ages six to twelve, should be at the "concrete operations" stage of Piaget's cognitive development theory, which is characterized by the ability to think and solve problems through logical and coherent actions. They grasp the principles of permanence and conservation by understanding that despite changes in external appearance, volume, weight, and numbers can remain constant. These kids should be able to draw on their previous experiences to explain why certain things happen. Their attention span should improve as they become older, going from about 15 minutes at age six to an hour at age nine.

Adolescents between the ages of 12 and 18 should be in Piaget's "formal operations" stage of cognitive development. It is characterized by a greater ability to think through problems and circumstances on one's own. Pure abstractions, such as philosophy and higher math concepts, should be understandable to adolescents. Children should be able to learn and use general information to adapt to specific situations at this age. They should also be able to learn the specialized knowledge and abilities required for a particular job. A cognitive transition is an important part of the adolescent experience. Adolescents think in ways that are more mature, efficient, and complex than children's thinking. There are five ways to look at this talent.

References: -

- www.healthofchildren.com/C/Cognitive-Development.html/cognitive-
- https://dataworks-ed.com/blog/2014/08/concept-development-what-it-is
- https://www.yogiraj.co.in/Explain-principles-of-growth-and-development/
- https://www.preservearticles.com/education/the-following-are-the-important/

VIII

ADJUSTMENT CONCEPT PROCESS OF ADJUSTMENT AND DEFENCE MECHANISM

Dr. Abhishek Srivastava, *Associate Professor, Faculty of Management Studies,* Gopal Narayan Singh University, Rohtas, Bihar
Swati singh, *Student, Guru Nanak Dev. Institute of Technology, Delhi. B.Voc. Software Development*

Introduction

In science, adjustment refers to the activity method by that humans and alternative animals accomplish a balance between their various needs or between their demands and therefore the difficulties in their circumstances. Once a necessity is felt, a series of changes begins and finishes with the satisfaction of that require. Hungry folks, as an example, ar compelled to hunt food by their state. They're acclimated to the current explicit demand after they eat as a result of the stimulating scenario that compelled them to action is reduced after they eat.

What is adjustment ?

The word "adjustment" comes from the word "adaptation" in biology. Biologists used the phrase "adaptation" to discuss with changes within the physical demands of the surroundings, whereas psychologists use the term "adjustment" to discuss with changes within the social or inter-personal relationships in society.

The individual's response to the stress and pressures of the social surroundings is noted as adjustment. The individual could also be needed to retort to associate external or internal demand.

Adjustment has been seen by psychologists from 2 perspectives: "adjustment as a goal" and "adjustment as a method."

Adjustment as achievement:

The term "adjustment as achievement" refers to a human ability to fulfil his job effectively in a very style of things. If we tend to contemplate adjustment to be a hit, we tend to should establish criteria to assess the standard of the adjustment. Psychologists have developed four criteria for judgment the adequacy of adjustment. the subsequent ar a number of them:

- Physical well-being
- Psychological ease
- Efficiency within the work and
- Acceptance in society

Adjustment as a process:

The phrase "adjustment as a process" emphasises the method by that an individual adjusts to his or her surroundings. It's essential, significantly from the attitude of academics. The degree to that students change is primarily determined by their interactions with the surroundings during which they live. They're perpetually trying to adapt to that. Jean Piaget checked out the adaptive method from a spread of views.

Assimilation and accommodation ar terms utilized by Jean Piaget to explain the method of adjusting oneself or one's surroundings.

Assimilator could be a one who retains his or her principles and standards of conduct no matter massive changes within the social atmosphere.

The term "accommodator" refers to somebody WHO adapts their concepts to the dynamic ideals of society by taking their standards from their social setting.

In order to with success integrate into society, an individual should use each devices, specifically assimilation and accommodation.

Characteristics of a well-adjusted person:

Some noticeable activity patterns ought to be gift in a very healthy and well-balanced person. These patterns of behaviour should be according to a human social expectations. the subsequent ar some samples of these patterns:

- Imaginative maturity
- Emotional equilibrium
- Others ar treated with heat and thought.
- Free from the strain of everyday occurrences
- Making selections on your own

Elements in adjustment:

There ar many key factors for meeting the wants that ar needed for a human healthy adjustment. the subsequent ar the details:

- Satisfaction of necessities
- There is no impediment to meeting desires.
- Strong motivations for meeting demands
- Possibility of an appropriate geographical surroundings to satisfy desires

Mechanisms of adjustment

Individuals use 'adjustment mechanisms' to regulate to their surroundings, solve difficulties, and touch upon the anxiety-inducing and conflicting processes of life. Any habitual strategy of overcoming blockages, accomplishing goals, satisfying reasons, easing frustration, and associated conserving physiological condition will be classified as an adjustment mechanism. Every person depends on his or her own mechanisms to stay the balance of his or her adjustment at intervals and toward society under control.

Defense mechanism

Any of a group of mental processes that allows the mind to succeed in compromise solutions to disputes that it's unable to resolve, in keeping with psychotherapy theory. The compromise is sometimes unconscious, and it entails concealment internal urges or sensations that threaten to undermine shallowness or cause anxiety from oneself. the thought is predicated on the psychotherapy theory that there square measure opposing forces within the mind that fight one different. Sigmund Freud coined the term in his study "The Neuro-Psychoses of Defense" (1894).

The following square measure a number of the main defence mechanisms delineated by psychoanalysts:

1. **Repression** is that the method of golf stroke associate degree unwelcome plan, affect, or need into the unconscious space of the mind so as to get rid of it from consciousness. A instance of hysterical cognitive state, within which the victim performs or witnesses a terrible act and later on entirely forgets concerning it and therefore the circumstances encompassing it, is associate degree example.

2. **Reaction** creation is that the acutely aware concentration on associate degree opposing thought, mood, or need to a feared unconscious impulse. as an example, a mother World Health Organization bears associate degree unwanted child might react to her guilt for not needing the kid by changing into protective and solicitous so as to steer each the kid and herself that she could be a smart mother.

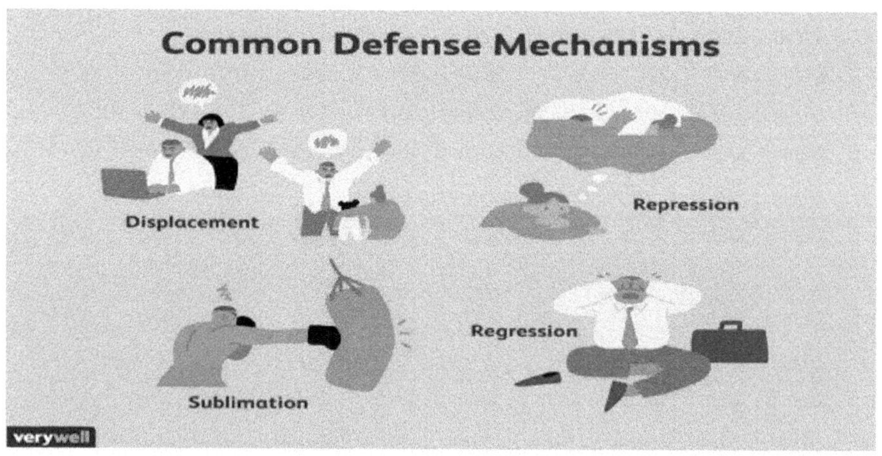

Source: very well

3. **Projection** could be a protecting mechanism within which unsought sentiments square measure projected onto another person, wherever they're perceived as a danger from the surface world. once a private is intimidated

by his own furious feelings, he accuses another of harbouring hostile concepts, that could be a common sort of projection.

4. **Regression** could be a comeback to earlier stages of development and abandoned forms of pleasure that square measure related to them, triggered by dangers or conflicts that arise at one in all the later stages.

After her first dispute with her husband, a young wife can retire to the safety of her parents' house.

5. **Sublimation** is the redirection of instinctive desires, usually sexual ones, into non-instinctual channels. According to psychoanalytic thought, the energy spent on sexual desires can be diverted to more socially acceptable and even productive pursuits, such as artistic or scientific endeavours.

6. **Denial** is the deliberate reluctance to acknowledge the existence of uncomfortable realities. An individual can avoid intolerable ideas, feelings, or experiences by suppressing hidden feelings of homosexuality or animosity, or mental problems in one's child.

The deployment of a defence mechanism is a normal element of personality function, according to psychoanalysts, and is not an indication of psychiatric disease in and of itself. Excessive or strict employment of these defences, on the other hand, can be a symptom of a variety of psychological illnesses.

CONCLUSION

For one thing, adjustment is a goal, and for another, it is a process. The first highlights the effectiveness or quality of adjustment, while the second emphasises the process by which an individual adjusts to his external environment. Thus, healthy adjustment is a process in which an individual successfully achieves his biological, psychological, and social requirements while also establishing a balance between his inner wants and society's outward demands through appropriate behavioural reactions.

REFERENCES

- https://www.britannica.com/science/photoperiodism
- http://www.edugyan.in/2017/03/adjustment-maladjustment.html
- https://www.britannica.com/topic/defense-mechanism
- esearchgate.net/publication/ 314087231_ADJUSTMENT_PROCESS_ACHEIVEMENT_
- CHARACTERISTICS_MEASUREMENT_AND_DIMENSIONS
- http://egyankosh.ac.in/bitstream/123456789/8519/1/Unit-16.pdf

- https://www.indiastudychannel.com/resources/131499-Types-of-adjustment-in-Psychology.aspx
- https://dictionary.apa.org/adjustment
- https://en.wikipedia.org/wiki/Adjustment_(psychology)
- https://www.simplypsychology.org/defense-mechanisms.html
- https://nptel.ac.in/content/storage2/courses/109104070/Module-1.pdf

IX

THE INVENTION OF CREATIVITY: THE EMERGENCE OF A DISCOURSE

Mr.Anand Prakash Dube,Associate Professor, School of Management Sciences,Varanasi.
Kanishka Tomar, Pupil Teacher, Manvi Institute of Education and Technology, SCERT.

INTRODUCTION

Creativity is increasingly cited as the key to social and economic change in the twenty-first century. It is also a very modern concept—making its first appearance as an English noun in 1875. This essay investigates the cultural construction of creativity in the context of the history of ideas. It understands creativity not as an innate human instinct or ability, but as an idea that emerges out of specific historical moments, shaped by the discourses of politics, science, commerce, and nation. It shifts the ground of analysis away from the naturalized models that have traditionally dominated the field of creative practice research, in order to highlight the historicity of a concept that is more commonly deemed to be without history.

Source: https://axiomq.com/

The investigations show if artists confronting substantial external limitations in their creativeness vary from artists who are free to decide on the subjects and resources, the time schedule, and so on in their notions of creation. Sixty-four artists from various fields of visual art have provided free definitions of creativity and classified the quality of products and individuals as characteristic of their unique creative definitions. As a control group were included 47 psychology students. Contents analyses of the free definitions and quantitative analysis of the classifications both revealed systematic distinctions between 'free' artists (for example painters or sculptors), more restricted artists (such as architects and designers), and psychological pupils. The one thing accepted by all the groups was for a creative individual to have numerous ideas. For example, we discovered disparity in terms of the relevance of a job for a creative product or the importance of a creative person's capacity to solve difficulties. Psychology students tended to highlight good sentiments produced by creative activity, although creativity was commonly called a hard effort for both groups of artists.

This section examines the subject of creativity in the artificial intelligence area (AI). Besides the uncertainties with respect to product, method or person, for four reasons, the definition of creativity is challenging. The first issue is that the notion requires a positive assessment. An concept that is considered innovative needs to be intriguing. This assessment typically relies on the variables of society and history and these assessments cannot be explained solely by psychological theory. The second issue is whether the author has to realise the worth of an idea to be referred to as creative. If so, someone with a good idea but who rejects it is not innovative. The third problem is the strain between historical (H) and psychological (P) sentiments. An thought is creative if it is innovative, even if others have previously had this concept in regard of the intellect. An concept is H-creative when it's P-creative and nobody has ever had the notion. Creativity with H is more glamorous, while creativity with P is more essential. The fourth difficulty is that only a few instances are covered by the usual operational definition. Many psychologists characterize the unique synthesis of common concepts as creativity. This is neither a distinction between P-News and H-News or an assessment. Two definitions of creativity are therefore needed, both of which need an intriguing new concept. The creativity of improbability involves new and unlikely pairings of old concepts. Novel thoughts that the individual could not have had before regarding the current domain conventions relate to the impossibility or exploratory-transformation creativity. These two creative kinds are described in this chapter and AI models are discussed in relation to arts and science.

While creativity may enhance the unity of approach only as a uniqueness, usefulness and surprise, the same definition shows that creativity can diminish in seven distinct ways. These options have been recognized :

(a) fortunate bias in response,

(b) irrational perseverance;

(c) problem discovery;

(d) rational removal,

(e) irrational removing; and

(f) blissful ignorance. Routine or reproductive or customable concepts.

In addition to giving a more detailed understanding of creative failure, the term has important implications for the processes and processes necessary to create highly innovative ideas.

CONCEPT OF CREATIVITY

Source: https://static3.depositphotos.com/

In all parts of life, creativity is an important idea, because creative individuals assure development. However, a strong definition of creativity is still lacking. This was not a significant concern in the 1950s since creative research was restricted to creative individuality and the process of creative thinking. As the 20th century proceeded, the study area was divided and a broad range of definitions of creativity were established. As a single definition is required for practical study into a concept, a new examination of the idea of creativity has to be undertaken in the 21st century. Creativity is an important notion in all areas of life since creative people ensure growth. However, there is currently no solid definition of creativity. This was not relevant in the 1950s, since creative study was limited to creative uniqueness and the creative thought process. With the course of the 20th century, the subject of research was separated and a wide variety of creativity definitions were defined. A new inquiry into the idea of creativity must be done in the 21st century since a single definition is needed for a concrete research on a topic. Every word supplied as a response was considered to have a significant connection with creativity both in the first and second studies. The outcome was a 42-word list. In the third and most significant research, the remaining 42 words were split into groups or categories by a fresh set of students. The card-sorting approach was used: Each participant was given 42 words in individual cards, which he was instructed to sort in groups. The rationale for the categorization was deliberately kept unclear, so the participants had to name the groups. This approach has often included certain terms whilst no participants have put other words together. The more often they put together two terms, the deeper the connection between them. An analysis of the Hierarchical Cluster was used to disclose the strengths of all these linkages. This might lead to the formation of groupings of words. The eight components of creativity provide the most essential conclusion to this theory. A comparison analysis using a different measurement technique of association strength was carried out to check the outcomes of the investigations. This study demonstrated that the varied ways of evaluating the strengths of the connection were unexpectedly unlike many. The discussion section provides possible causes for this difference. In naming the creativity components, the conclusion of the thesis may be demonstrated: - Originality - Emotion - Inventiveness - Process - Intellectuality - Hobby - Practice.

In this article, two corporations of the literature examine recent research on the notion of creativity in two cultures—the Eastern (Asian) cultures and the Western (European and US). One is on people's implied creativity theories via different cultures and the other about cross-cultural creativity research. Studies on implicit creative ideas in the East reveal that many Asians have many individuals in the West who have similar but not identical views of creativity. Cross-cultural creativity research indicate that East and West differ in their differing thought and creative manifestations on average. It presents a concept of creativity as largely culture-specific and discusses the suitability of utilizing diverging thought tests to assess creativity.

The idea of creativity is challenged for being too loosely defined and overly influenced by an operationalist approach from below. It is also said that current popular creative definitions do not separate creativity from traditional concepts of intelligence, which likewise rely on novelty and adequacy as essential characteristics, by emphasizing on originality and suitability.

This conceptual issue is solved by clearly distinguishing the novelty on the stimulus from the novelty on the response side. This distinction is utilized as a foundation to create a new taxonomy of creativity and intelligent behavior of different sorts. The difference between proactive and reactive creativity is an important characteristic of this new approach. In conclusion, the conceptual model is utilized to identify some deficiencies in existing creative tests and to provide certain proposals with regard to the architecture of a new type of creativity evaluation taking account of a practical-educational viewpoint.

Proposes that validation of the idea of an ordinarily distributed characteristic for creativity should be positively linked in unselected samples to traits that separate famous creatives from less eminent individuals. The notion is not clearly supported by an assessment of the existing evidence. Taken along with previous data, this finding shows that a divergent thought should not be considered creative. Discuss creativity as a voyage since it needs attention and may involve key moments that disturb or discontinue creativity. The creative path has 7 processes: framing, testing, explore, revalue, reinforce, reframe and realize. In every step there is a shift in the connection of the pursuer to the phenomena and fresh perspectives are obtained.

PROCESS OF CREATIVITY

Source: https://image.shutterstock.com/

At least four components are creativity:
(1) creative output,
(2) creative individual and
(3) creative scenario
(4) creation output;

Theoretical views, each having its own assumptions, methods, biases, and even meta-theory perspectives have been examined from so many sometimes-contradictory angles that it is not feasible to address all in one chapter. This chapter focuses on the divergent approach to the analysis of the creative process, which has the best theoretical basis, most creativity tests and the most empirical research. In addition, information will be given on some additional components and theoretical methods. Creativity in various fields is seen in different ways: it is referred to as 'innovation' in education, 'entrepreneurship' in business, typically referred to as 'problem solving' in mathematics and 'performance' or 'composition' in music. A creative output in diverse fields with its own laws, techniques and concepts of creativity are assessed against the standards of that domain.

Learning, however, is made of both product and process in every academic area. Although in many fields the output might be fairly diverse, there are common pedagogical concepts that promote process creativity. 'Creative teaching' might be called the creation of a learning environment that encourages students to see both the essence and the subject details, to formulate and resolve problems, to look at the connectivity between different fields, to take up and to respond to new ideas and to include the element of surprise in their work. Such a learning environment includes not just suitable resources, but also learning approaches that address the crucial emotive elements of creativity.

Her goods have been the most popular method of detecting creativity. The presence of a creative output is a precondition for considering creativity in architecture, music, literature, art, even problem resolving and scientific discovery. Alternatively, anecdotal accounts were utilized to identify creative processes. Many scientific findings have been associated with an unexplained insight or revelation, marked by the AHA! Response. Apart from the creative output itself and the answer from AHA! There are several forms of physical proof that show the creative process. Our objective is to study these phenomenon's further and to create ideas on the nature of the creative process. Our ultimate objective is to build a broad creativity theory. This idea is based on the circumstances needed for the creative process in a variety of fields: riddles, scientific discoveries, design with a particular focus on architectural design.

Hypothesizes that creative activity is a particular way of connecting the primary and secundary processes, in which the loose, illogical and highly subjective concept of the primary process generates a new thought or insight. This is then shaped into a setting that is socially relevant and relevant to others through a subsequent process. Although evidence of creativity is poor by the degree of primary process involvement reveals how creative capabilities connect to the extent to which the secondary process starts integrative control over the manifestations of primary processes.

There is a discussion about the difference between science and art. It is also described how certain creative styles may depend on the direct access to primary-process thought by the secondary process, while other styles may entail the usage in creation of particular functions from the secondary process.

ROLE OF SCHOOL IN FOSTERING CREATIVITY

Source: https://centaur-wp.s3.eu-central-1.amazonaws.com/

Despite composition's inclusion in music curriculum in the UK, USA, Canada and Australia, it remains a fragmented and challenging problem to grasp the function of creativity for composing in schools. The purpose of this article is to rely on an international understanding of the makeup of individual pupils from different origins. This research is aimed at developing instructional techniques that may encourage creativity during composition. Over the last five years, the focus for policymakers in education has been on innovation. However, there has been an upsurge in interest in creativity, with no relation to the value system. This essay contends that Western individualism, in turn, supported as well as led by the worldwide capitalist market, really supplied an unseen underlying value framework. What may this imply to promote creativity in classrooms with wisdom?

This book provides more inspirational insight and encourages instructors to appreciate a more diverse array of abilities, with special emphasis on creativity, novelty, discovery and so on. Techniques and methods are proposed in the classroom to promote risky and innovative thinking. It is also, and maybe particularly crucial for creativity, important that teachers be clear in understanding the emotional and motivational foundation of learning and thinking to focus on its cognitive components not simply. Therefore the book is anticipated that the vast variety of elements in the classroom that influence conventional as well as creative thinking will be more fully understood.

Initially, education concerns drive the increase in interest in creativity after the Sputnik shock in the 1950s. These focused on the notion that schools and colleges produced huge numbers of graduates, but most of them were educated to use the traditional methods previously known. The proposal that features required for creativity are helpful to develop by providing adequate learning environments deliberately supports creativity in schools.

This chapter focuses on identifying what instructors should encourage and use concepts for this purpose. Two Many instructors and parents are uncomfortable with the emphasis on school creativity since that may encourage disobedience, disobedience, carefree conduct or just uncertainty. Others perceive a demand for innovation in the classroom to be permitted by any behavior and forsake essential skills, norms, and principles such as right or wrong. All children and young people experience the processes and personal properties involved in promoting creativity in the lesson and promoting creativity helps all pupils, not only the handful that are renewed as renowned innovators. From the beginning we should also realise that the aim to encourage creativeness is an integral element of an educational heritage which goes back to ancient Greeks at least.

Many creative training methods appear to only increase performance for activities directly related to training. Rump (1979) found in a thorough examination on data that, when the criteria closely match the training process, the impact of training is highest and worst when this resemblance is modest. Only limited impacts (as opposed to thinking) are achieved in the case of personalities, interests and preferences. As a result, it may be concluded that training processes affect attitudes, values, self-image or motivation minimally. It is also possible to have a contrary impact from the targeted creative education. For example, students could become aware that some types of conduct are favored by the instructor and that the teacher could change his/her approach to issues appropriately. While the education can motivate youngsters to work hard on many tasks, they can learn that "original" responses are easily provided by division of hair, ranging replies without regard to correctness or relevancy, or delivering surprising tricks. The creative process does not depend on any unique abilities, which can be acquired in math like tables, in much the same manner that specialist bodybuilding can be created. What is necessary is to promote creativity through specific techniques of teaching and learning spread over the full curriculum.

WHAT SHOULD TEACHERS FOSTER?

Source: https://static.babyandchild.ae/

Early creativity studies mostly focused on creative thought (see specifics later). It became abundantly obvious, however, that kids show only inventiveness if and when they choose to. In addition, youngsters must be able to identify discrepancies and generate suggestions, for example. The subsequent parts will examine these characteristics of creativity in greater depth. The key components of this constellation need to be outlined at that time, as these are the processes and qualities that instructors must encourage in the classroom to foster creative development. Learners should regard the collection of knowledge, certain methods of thinking, inventiveness in discovering answers, the capacity to assess ideas, the ability to convey solutions to other people and the evaluation of real-world solutions as fundamental components of creativity. Taylor (1975) 9 also gave insights on the distinction between truly (the actually startling) creative and other types of novelty. Five degrees of creativity were described:

(a) technical creativity is seen with exceptional linguistics, tools, tools of trade, tools and such like,

(b) inventive creativity involves using in an innovative fashion what has been known;

(c) innovative creativity takes place where known principles or paradigms are employed to develop new ideas; and

(d) emergent creativity; and

(e) innovative creativity;

Dillon (1982) indicates that there are three challenges:

(a) identification of evident problems on the basis of field knowledge;

(b) identification of hidden difficulties on the basis of concentrated effort in the area; and

(c) inventing problems because existing information is reorganized.

Teachers are familiar with defining the difficulties students are faced with and assessing to what degree the answers of students match with the proper answer that is commonly known to the teacher in advance. Convergent thinking is applying conventional logic to a number of information components in order to include the one and only optimal solution suggested by the information available—the response which would have come from anyone who had the same stock and who applied the principles of conventional logic. Since the solution is unique and develops more or less unavoidably from the information given, it already exists and should only be discovered in a particular sense. Divergent thought, on the other hand, entails answering by deviating, for example, from the given knowledge, by perceiving unforeseen elements that other people could not see. Knowledge in the field is the reason for recognizing such gaps (Birch, 1975). The following summarizes the results of this study on the cognitive elements of creativity for teachers. In their pupils they should aim to promote:

1 Fund of general knowledge possession.

2 One or more particular areas of knowledge.

3 An active imagination.

4 Ability to identify, find or invent issues.

5 Ability to recognize linkages, overlaps, parallels, and logical consequences (convergent thinking).

6. Competency to create distant relationships, to combine, to accept main process material, to create new designs, etc. (divergent thinking).

7. Ability to find several solutions to issues.

8. A lodging choice, not assimilation

9. Capacity to share results with other people.

10. Ability and desire to review their own work.

FOSTERING CREATIVITY

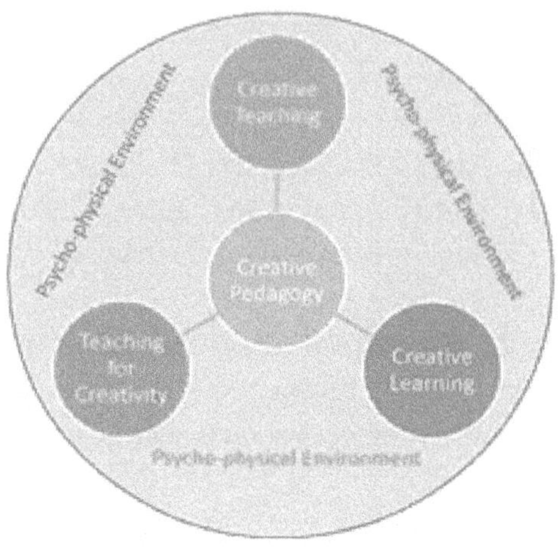

Source: https://www.semanticscholar.org/

Teachers must not only aim to offer releasers but also to remove blockages to encourage creativity. The recently given conclusions combining resumes like Cropley 19 (1992a) and Torrance (1992) recommend that teachers should provide importance and support to qualities like:

1. Task commitment, tenacity and resolve
2. Independence and non-compliance
3. Trust and willingness to risk being mistaken.
4. Take the lead and tackle tough things willingly.

This might be spoken sooner than done, as teachers typically chew on creative features. Research has revealed that many teachers do not enjoy these features. In the United States (for example, Bachtold, 1974) as well as in other jurisdictions more recent research corroborated earlier Torrance results (1970) in this regard (Howieson, 1984; Obuche, 1986; Raina, 1972). Stone (1980) discovered that two grades pupils with the greatest creative scores had been evaluated as the most commonly troublesome among instructors by their peers. It may be queried how the feedback teachers offer creative pupils if they consider their conduct to be undisciplined, unruly, distrustful or even humiliating. However, there is proof of teachers' support for creativity, overwhelming in the classroom,—Feldhusen and Treffinger

(1975) claim that 96% of instructors have taken this position. The issue seems to be the recognition of 'immature' creative potential versus the recognition of creative potential; definitely, many teachers are often confronted by really disruptive behavior. Again, the problem of identifying and separating signs of creative potential from misconduct is highlighted here. 20 In this respect, an intriguing result is that creative professors prefer to provide creative pupils greater assistance. Milgram (1979) showed that instructor creativity and student creativity correlated. McLeod and Cropley (1989) referred to professors who look particularly comfortable with creative pupils as "creativity nurturing." As Cropley (1982) has pointed out, these teachers provide a model of creative behaviour, strengthen such behavior, while students demonstrate it, protect creative students against pressure of conformity from their peers, provide safe refuge for their students, when they are ridiculed and criticized by other peers, parents or professors. Cropley (1982) reports that people that promote creativity are the teachers:

1 Encourage students to learn independently

2 Have a cooperative, socially integrated teaching approach

3 Ensure that their pupils have a good basis for diverse thinking.

4 Facilitate flexible thinking in students

5 Foster self-assessment in students

6 Take student suggestions and questions seriously

7 Offer student's opportunities to work with various materials and under a variety of different conditions.

8 Deliver the students' ideas until they are carefully developed and clearly formulated

9 Help pupils get the confidence to try out new and odd things to cope with frustration and frailty.

CONCLUSION

Discusses diversity in evolution and features of creative selection. Selection mechanisms at the level of ideas, individual producers and communities or civilizations are explored. Cognitive selection, interpersonal and sociocultural selection are the factors explored. These variables reflect restrictions on many levels to limit the world's ideational diversity. Problem identification restrictions placed on solution generation by creative persons and limitations. In conclusion, the following topics are stressed:

(1) Creativity is a risky activity;

(2) Creativity is threatened by the adjustment of trade-offs; and

(3) Achieving a balance between opposites is frequently a result of curvilinear relationships between historical and creative factors.

REFRENCES

Floor, M. A. (1996). Creativity. With Artificial Intelligence (pp. 267-291). Academic press. Academic press.

Holzmann, M., Schmidt, S., & Unger, F. (2002). How creatives describe creativity: Definitions represent many creativity kinds. Reporters Without Borders, 14(1), 55-67.

Merchant, D. K. (2018). Defining creativity: do we not have to describe that which is not creative, too? Creative Conduct Journal, 52(1), 80-90.

Mann, J., & Karlsruhe, M. (2002). Contemporary research on the creative concept: Eastern and Western. Creative Comportement Journal, 36(4), 269-288.

Builder, G. (2003). What should be measured? A new view on the creative concept. Education Research Journal, 47(3), 235-251 of the Scandinavian Government.

M. Ben, J. G. J. (1972). The creativeness of the individual who never creates anything fresh and helpful: the notion of creativity as a feature usually distributed. Psychologist of America, 27(8), 717.

Müller-Wienbergen, F., Müller, S., & Becker, J. (2010). The notion of creativity in the discipline of information systems: past, present and future. Information Systems Association communication, 27(1), 14. Communications.

Robinson, K. (1982). Extend the creative concept. The Creative Conduct Journal.

Michel, R. A. (2014). Defining the creativity idea (Twente University, Master's degree).

Petocz, M., & Reid, A. (2004). The fields of learning and creativity process. Australian Researcher for Education, 31(2), 45-62.

Karl, J., & Krads, M. (1998). The creative process in puzzles, innovations and designs. Building automation, 7(2-3), 123-138.

Oh, Oh, J. R. (1980). Thought and creativity primary process. Newsletter on Psychology, 98(1), 144.

Brown, R. T. Brown, R. (1989). Creativity. In the Creativity Manual (pp. 3-32). Boston, MA, Springer.

Alice, J., & Karlsruhe, A. (2002). Pathways to map: Encouraging composition creativity. Research on Music Education, 4(2), 245-261.

Karl, A. J. (1992). More than one way: to promote creativity. Editing of Ablex.

Handwerk, A. (2006). Encouraging wisdom in creation. Education Journal, 36(3), 337-350 in Cambridge.

Karl, A. J. (1997). Encouraging classroom creativity: general concepts. 1(84.114), 1-46. The Creative Research Manual.

Claude, D. Aleppo (2003). Creativity as change and selection: certain key restrictions.

X

THE CONCEPT OF INTELLIGENCE: USEFUL OR USELESS?

Kanishka Tomar, Pupil Teacher, Manvi Institute of Education and Technology, SCERT.

INTRODUCTION

There is no history in the field of intelligence, but several histories depending on who says the narrative. Carroll, Herrenstein, Murray and Jensen, for example, have recounted the laudative storey somewhat differently from the most questionable tales of Gardner, Gould, Lemann, Sacks or Stanovich. Perhaps more balanced stories are Mackintosh's. Of course, there are differences in these categories of authors. These variations must be noted as while the ideological lenses are used in many fields of psychology, few areas seem to have lens colors, and some could claim that there are a lot of various flaws, such as lenses, in which understanding is observed. The different perspectives derive from the ideological preconceptions which not only influence statements but also the inclusive. For instance, Carroll versus Gardner nearly overlaps historic data used to support their conflicting intelligence ideas. In this chapter I investigate three methods to clarification of values, but there can be no genuine value-free account. First, I try to convey the views of researchers and their eras throughout the history of the subject. . Secondly, I analyse this work by pinpointing evolutional aspects and revealing what my own ideas are.

Thirdly, I am dialectically seeking to represent many points of view which emphasize both the positive and the negative side of various contributions. It is understood that in the future all points of view taken in the past might be regarded as being warped by "20/20 retrospectives."

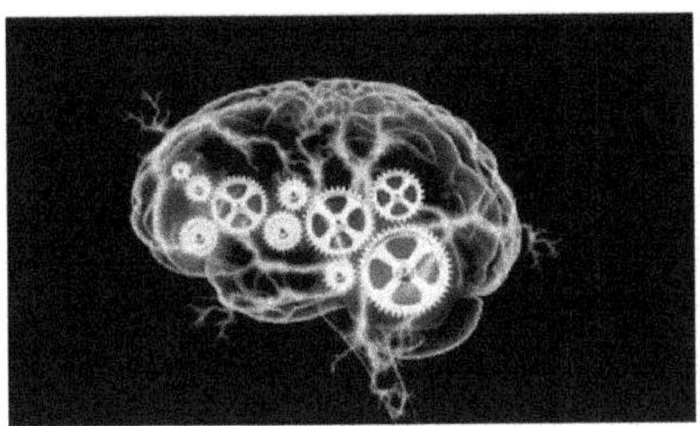

Source: https://lh3.googleusercontent.com/

A dialectic examination will be used for the full chapter. The basic premise is that good or bad core ideas are eventually a springboard for new ideas, which have developed from the previously inconsistent relations between prior ideas. This chapter focuses on the history of intelligence, in particular intelligence theories. Contemporary thinking is referenced elsewhere, as is research interesting readers. These hypotheses and research are only discussed in passing in this chapter.

Intelligence suggestions that are better understood by examining non-inclusive (i.e. novel) issues, which need Ss to utilize other concepts or form techniques. The limited successful intelligence techniques in cognitive and cognitive components are thought to be partially due to the use of more (known) tasks than they are best suited for intelligence study.

After reviewing Harlow's work on the "learning sets," the author examined the historical and empirical bases for the notion of "fixed information" and "pre-defined development" and obtained insight into Hebb's core processes, the actions of computers and programmers. In the framework of the continuing commitment with his environment, Piaget's studies on sensory motors and successive stages are examined and evaluated.

The child develops logical procedures. The authors then assess parts of Piaget's work on psychological theories in light of new ideas and facts, and try certain Piaget's notions to prove established intelligence and predictable growth.

CONCEPT OF INTELLIGENCE

The theory of ideas of Rosch, applied by the idea of intelligence, points to the fact that one's intelligence resembles one prototypically intelligent individual. Since no characteristic feature is the prototype, a process-based intelligence definition cannot be stated appropriately. As a rule, combining numerous experimental measurements into a single index, such in a Binet test, would be appropriate. In fact, it is just difficult to measure many of the important traits. His paper provides a definition of intelligence that includes the mental ability to adapt to, and to pick and shape, any environment. Although the conduct described as intelligent may change from one environmental situation to another, the mental processes behind this activity are not. According to this definition. However, the capacity of an individual to use these procedures may vary from one setting to another. The capacity is used to achieve exterior world correspondence and internal coherence between diverse systems of knowledge and belief. There is a discussion on the usefulness of the concept to comprehend contemporary theories, intelligence tests, and the function of intelligence in lifelong learning.

This editorial discusses current developments in intelligence, especially with regard to response times and the average evocative potential based on experimental evidence. First, it was claimed that the notion of a general intelligence factor should not be abandoned, as many contemporary researchers have shown. It is not just valuable but also necessary in terms of explaining empirical evidence provided through confirmation factor analyses, multidimensional scale, and so on. In addition, attempts to explain the difference between the learning, cultural and environmental and educational variables in cognitive operation cannot be held accountable for recent evidence that exhibits high correlations between basic physiological (evocated) potential (effect times, movement times, inspection times) and perceptual motor processes (IQ). The controversy about the meaning of intelligence was largely caused by the incapacity to meet threefold intelligence criteria and the fact that summarized experimental evidence and theoretical issues should be considered in any acceptable theory. These have produced a "fresh appearance" in the notion of intelligence (Eysenck, 1986).

TYPES OF INTELLIGENCE

The ideas of implicit intelligence were investigated with exemplary intelligence surveys. Examination 1 was a four-sample study of remarkable cases. These different samples showed similar numbers of popular specimens split into five groups. There were five forms of intelligence: science, art, business, communication and moral intelligence. Study 2 has rejected the idea that, because of the little overlap between intelligence and the tales of famousness, inventiveness and wisdom, the example stories are both indiscriminate and available. In Study 3, 50 famous persons were evaluated as compared with individual intellectual specimens. The popularity of each five ratings was outstanding. 31 percent were not known for outstanding Study 4 reports include not just famous people (friends, family members, teachers, etc.). The data demonstrate that five implied types of intellect play a role in people's ideas, each highly available.

Scientific Intelligence

During World War II, scientist intelligence was coined, but despite its antiquity and relative importance it has not received the respect it should have had. The interest in the WMD programmes is unexpectedly growing recently. The key components of scientific intelligence are presented in This essay, aiming to investigate the definition and functioning of scientific intelligence and its significant problems. This seeks to establish an agenda in this crucial subject for future study.

Artistic Intelligence

In the financial, medicinal and educational industries, machinery learning (ML) is used to develop smart stock forecasts, health robots and virtual support, for instance. However, its usage has mainly not been used by the artistic expression in one of the most human endeavors. Present ML applications in creative projects use primarily artificial agents in order to enhance human capability to regions where huge data have access to untapped human artists' connections. These examples initially look at human beings and only enhance human ability to build new musical combinations based on a basic range of tones, to analyse photographic material to pick styles for future image modifications or to combine poetic language based on phonetic similarities, for example. While ML is employed in such applications as a data mining agent for unknown domains, it does not exceed the predicted human constraints. In everything with which we engage, we use Artificial intelligence (AI) in unexpected ways, another field in which the ML enables artistic expression. Imagine talking, for example, to a guy who responds with Google Assistant or to a robotic person who wants to use drugs secretly. I recommend using ML to generate new behavior such that unknown preset training settings for users can modify these behaviors. The application of ML to unexpected types of interaction alters what computers we think are able to do. They provide occasions in which the meaning of intelligence for mankind transcends beyond human assumptions.

ENTREPRENURIAL INTELLIGENCE

The entrepreneur has identified entrepreneurial research as a catalyst for the new entrepreneurial process. The study of the emotional intelligence of business executives was a popular line of research that has not yet been applied to entrepreneurship. This web-based study collected emotional skills data on successful young entrepreneurs. Participating entrepreneurs indicated high standards of self-assurance, confidence, performance direction, service orientation, a catalyst for change, cooperation and collaboration. Confidence, the capacity to retain norms of integrity and honesty, rated best among 18 tested emotional skills. The findings also stress the significance of teamwork and partnership in the new venture process.

Communicative Intelligence

In the unexpectedly dynamic field of human interaction CI is the purposeful and intentional use of verbal and nonverbal models of communication so as to create links across cultures and civilizations (see Zoller, 2008). Moreover, the author believes that CI is a deliberately conscious condition where verbal and nonverbal abilities and motions are utilized to match the message with the way in which relationships, model empathy and trust in impact are viewed. By adopting CI's techniques and approaches, leaders may improve the quality of their relations, leading to new opportunities and solutions to the problems that companies face. Key themes of interest, including how CI may influence intercultural collaboration and leadership, will be explored.

Moral Intelligence

Moral intelligence is newer and less researched, but it has a tremendous potential to increase our knowledge of learning and behaviour than existing cognitive, emotional and social intelligentsia. The capacity to apply ethical concepts to individual objectives, beliefs and behaviours is moral understanding. The structure of moral intelligence consists of four competences, three competences, forgiveness and compassion. Morally intelligent school leaders and instructors will encourage, respect and care for their kids and provide rise to them. This article explores what morals are and how leaders, teachers and children may be taught. It will be discussing its link with character and ethical conduct, and the other intelligences. The development of increased moral intelligence will lead to more constructive organizations, better connections and pupils who are both intelligent and decent, and who appreciate universal human rights and ideals.

THEORIES OF INTELLIGENCE

Guilford's Structure of Intellect

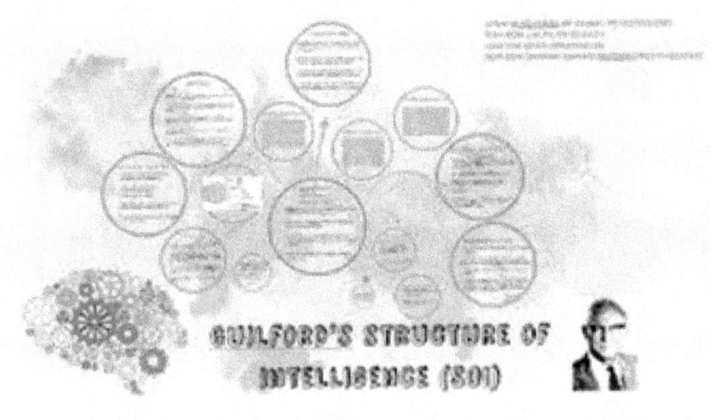

Source: https://encrypted-tbn0.gstatic.com/

J. P. Guilford was extremely influential in creative psychology. He is the father of contemporary creative research in many respects. Yet in certain aspects, we propose, his idea of creativity was faulty. In this essay we explore both Guilford's approach to creativity's benefits and limits. Theory shows that Procrustean methods of factoring may be utilized to deliver results which appear to support randomly defined hypotheses. This can be achieved even though:

(a) variables have been confidential and probably inter-related legally;

(b) orthogonal loading of factors;

(c) interpretation factor loadings have to be at least .30; and

(d) S samples are as large as 175, 205 and 240.

Results are understood to indicate a lack of convincing factor-analytic support to the SI theory since this is not significantly better than support for random-generated theories.

In the framework of capitalization on chance, the structure-of-intellect (SI) Theory is assessed. In the study of human intelligence, this empiric difficulty is brought within a broader view of the general conceptual usefulness of theory. There were numerous remarkable aspects of the analytical factor support for theory. At most, studies to support the concept should be seen as experimental. However, the model provided an effective strategy for testing and for showing intriguing ideas regarding intellectual characteristics. However, there are several difficulties with theory even in this situation. The idea simply gives a static taxonomy and hence provides extremely little opportunity to analyse developmental problems.

Howard Gardener's Theory

Source: https://cdn2.slidemodel.com/

New and more contextualized cognitive tasks are proposed as alternatives to more standard psychometric tests in the multiple intelligence paradigm. The aim of this essay is to explore whether or not these two sorts of devices converge into a generic cognitive component. A set of Gardner's multiple intellectual appraisal tasks, (language, logical, visual/spatial, body kinesthetic, naturalistic and musical intelligence), were administered to 294 children aged 5 to 7, including the battery of general and differential aptitudes (BADyG: reasoning, memory, oral aptitude, numerical aptitude and spatial aptitude). The confirmatory factor analysis shows that both batteries are without a single general factor, showing instead the presence of two general factors that collect the tests they include. Moreover, th

Source: https://cdn.slidesharecdn.com/

ese 2 general variables are consistent with traditional and multiple intelligence evaluations and demonstrate a statistically modest connection. These results contradict the initial stance of Gardner to refuse a generic intelligence component, especially in the context of measurements that do not correspond to more typical intelligence tests.

Gardner says it contains seven different intellectual units in the human organism. He identifies these units with their respective intelligences which are seen and quantifiable. The intellect hypothesis of Gardner is investigated in the framework of g, whereas the work of cognitive style theoreticians compares Gardner's Ml theory. This research indicates that Ml theory did not find new "intelligences," but revised what other people classified as cognitive styles.

Goleman's Emotional Intelligence

The principles from Daniel Goleman's book are brought to work using Emotional Intelligence. Corporate leaders and leading performers are identified not by their IQs or their talents, but via their "emotional intelligence." These are a series of abilities that differentiate how individuals are managing, interacting and communicating their feelings. Dozens of specialists in 500 companies, government agencies and NGOs throughout the world have analyzed the barometer of excellence in almost all jobs. This book discusses what is emotional intelligence and why it matters for excellence in the work more than IQ or knowledge. It contains 12 individual skills (e.g., correct self-evaluation, self-control, initiative and optimism) and 13 essential relational skills (such as service orientation, developing others, conflict management, and building bonds). Goleman contains several instances and storey from Fortune 500 to non-profit pre-school, showing how these skills are leading to or countering success.

Emotional intelligence includes a range of qualities including self-control, enthusiasm and tenacity. The key elements of anger, conflict management, empathy development, and impulses must be taught to every kid. Schools must support youngsters in their emotions recognition and management. In caring, respectful relationships with kids, educators should demonstrate emotional intelligence.

CONCLUSION

Research with delayed children and adults is one way of studying intelligence. Any definition of how they vary from non-retarded persons leads to a specification of essential intelligence components. We discuss two main topics of inquiry in this paper. One is that study with the retarded has managed to discover a key element of intelligence, centered on the role of control processes in memory and problem solving circumstances. The results of numerous experiments led us to the conclusion that intelligence is a hallmark for generalizing information from one state to the next and this ability depends on efficient "executive monitoring." We suggest that comparative/developmental work is necessary to gain a better knowledge in areas where fewer late-film research has been done. We demonstrate this by debating some work aimed at identifying individual parameter variations reflecting fundamental components of generic information processing systems.

To anticipate our ultimate conclusion, we support an intelligence perspective based on the executive of the invention and implementation of planning activities which can light the evolution of general theory in a major portion of intelligence.

REFRENCES

Oddson, R. J. (2013). Intelligence. Wiley & Sons Inc. John Inc.

J. M. Hunt. Hunt (1961). Smartness and expertise.

Oddson, R. J. (1981). Smartness and no tranquilization. Psychological Education Journal, 73(1), 1.

Nietz, U. (1979). The intelligence idea. Smart, 3(3), 217-227.

Oddson, R. J. (1997). The intelligence notion and its significance in lifelong learning and achievement. Psychologist from the United States, 10(52), 1030.

Odds, M. J. J. (1988). "Intelligence" concept: useful or ineffective? Smart, 12(1), 1-16.

L., Wehr, P., Harms, P. D., & Richmond, D. I. (2002). Exemplary surveys have been used to disclose implicit intelligence kinds. Bulletin on Humanity and Social Psychology, 28(8), 1051-1062.

Goodman. - Goodman, M. S. (2009). The paradigm of Jones: how, why, and why scientific intelligence. National Security Intelligence, 24(2), 236-256.

Michael, M. (2020). Critikos. Artistic Intelligence.

S. & White, R. J. Rhee, K. S. (2007). Entrepreneurs' emotional intelligence. Little Entrepreneurship Journal, 20(4), 409-425.

Customs, C. C. (2015). The ideology promoting cross-cultural collaboration by employing communication intelligence. Intercultural partnership and leadership in modern enterprises (pp. 303-320). Overall IGI.

Sky, R. H. R. (2009). Moral school-based intelligence. Entry online.

Müll, A., & Krausch, M. L. J. (2001). Intellectual model and creative model structure of Guilford: Contributions and constraints. Review of Creativity, 13(3-4), 309-316.

Knapp, J. L., & Horn, J. L. (1973). About the subjective nature of the empirical foundation of Guilford's intellectual framework.

Hans, J. O. & Klaus, J. L. J. (1977). Guilford's critical assessment of intellect-structure theory. Smart, 1(1), 65-81.

Almeida, L. S., M. D., Klaus, M. A., R. M., Holm, R., M. & Krebz, J. M. (2010). Assessment of intelligence: the Gardner hypothesis of multiple intelligence. Individual differences in learning and learning, 20(3), 225-230.

Morgan, H. - Morgan, H. (1996). Gardner's multiple intelligence theory is analysed. Review, 263-269, 18(4).

Goleman, D. Goleman, D. (1998). Emotional intelligence working.

O'Neil, J. Alice (1996). Emotional Intelligence: a talk to Daniel Goleman. Leadership of education, 54(1), 6-11. Education.

J. C., & Brown, A. L. S. (1978). Intelligence theory: contributions from delayed children's study. Caution, 2(3), 279-304.

XI
LANGUAGE DEVELOPMENT IN LEARNERS

Divine Tomar, Pupil Teacher, Manvi Institute of Education And Technology,SCERT

INTRODUCTION

The formation of a language is a fascinating process. In truth, learning language is a natural process that all newborns are born knowing how to do.1 interestingly, all children learn language in the same way, regardless of the language their parents speak. A child's ability to communicate and develop depends on his or her ability to use language. These abilities allow youngsters to interact with others and learn from their environment as well as in the classroom. Human beings are storytellers. No other species, as far as we know, has the capacity for language and the ability to employ it in infinitely inventive ways. Opening a box a toddler says open; seeing a toy car in it she says car; taking the car out she says out; putting it on the floor she says down. In the world at large these little remarks do not command much attention. But to people interested in how children learn to talk, the first steps into language raise fascinating and difficult questions.

Source: www.raisingchildren.net.au

Learning the rules for putting words together in a way that expresses their thoughts and feelings, as well as understanding the meaning of both the written and spoken word, are essential language skills for youngsters. The use of language is one of the characteristics that distinguishes human cultures from animal societies. Language is an essential component of all human cultures and a potent social skill that we learn at a young age. The ability to solve complicated issues is a second characteristic of humans. Philosophers have debated whether these two capacities are related and, if so, what the nature of the relationship between language and thought is for centuries.

This dispute drew psychologists into it at the turn of the century, and it is still generating a lot of study today. The influence of culture in the study of language and mind is another factor to consider. When we learn another country's language, we notice that not only the vocabulary and grammar are different, but also the customs and traditions. Even the culture's views and ways of dealing with life can be different. On the nature of the relationship between language and thought, there are several points of view. To properly comprehend either language or thought, we must first comprehend how they grow and interact in the minds of infants.

Philosophers have long debated the origins of our uniquely human capacities to communicate and understand in complicated ways. However, the issue has only recently been the focus of significant scientific investigation. We are currently in the midst of a research boom in this area. Many significant developments in the study of language and cognitive development have occurred in the last two decades. The utterances of tiny infants are being gathered, examined, and incorporated into bigger theories of human cognition now more than ever before. The goal of this volume is to report on and remark on these developments. The end result is a collection of precise and persuasive models of language-thought relationships (particularly, meaning-concept relationships) as mirrored in a child's developing mind. Focusing on growth as a window into language-thought interactions has two distinct purposes. One reason for this is that children's actions reveal restrictions on language and thought. Examining the forms and meanings that children develop, as well as the errors they make, allows us to establish how languages and conceptual systems are bound.

Children must be able to learn all natural languages; as a result, children provide hints to what is universal, not only in syntax but also in semantics. Teachers teach language to their students at all levels. A kindergarten teacher can be concerned about how her students' sounds are evolving. A fifth-grade teacher might be stumped as to how he can help his kids understand their science textbooks. A social studies–language arts teacher in eighth grade can confront the issue of integrating a student with minimal English and formal schooling into his or her class. A high school math teacher might be unsure how to effectively assist her students in developing academic vocabulary. Language acquisition occurs without formal instruction and appears to follow a similar pattern in youngsters from very disparate cultures. Immersion in a linguistic setting is the most effective way to learn a language. Children are exposed to linguistic information even before they are born.

VIEWS OF CHOMSKY ON LANGUAGE DEVELOPMENT

Source : www.streetroots.org

One of the most well-known linguists of the twentieth century, **Noam Chomsky**, based his linguistic studies on philosophical concepts. Noam Chomsky is still regarded as one of the most prominent intellectuals of the modern era. His contributions to linguistics, psychology, philosophy, and politics have transformed our understanding of language, the mind, and human nature. Transformational Generative Grammar, which is based on mentalist philosophy, is his most significant contribution to linguistics. He rejects behaviourist psychology in favour of innatism in understanding language learning.

He maintains that a human kid can acquire a language because of the linguistic capacity with which the child is born, and that adult language use is primarily a mental activity. Chomsky's ideas sparked a language revolution known as the Chomskyan Revolution. Universal Grammar, according to him, is the part of language that is innate to human beings. In quest of a cognitive foundation, his philosophy leans heavily on rationality. His theory is a continuation of analytic philosophy, which emphasises the importance of language in philosophical inquiry. He'd be classified as an essentialist as well.

We are born with a tendency to study language, according to Noam Chomsky. His views of language acquisition suggest that humans are pre-wired to learn language and that they are born knowing the fundamental laws of language. The environment greatly influences many of the distinctive characteristics of every individual language structure. The theory of universal grammar, the view that language is intrinsic, and the notion that language learning happens throughout important developmental phases were all introduced by Chomsky as new ways of thinking about language. Chomsky's theory is based on the assumption that all languages have identical structures and rules (universal grammar), and that the fact that children learn language in the same way, and without much effort, suggests that we're born with the fundamentals already in our heads. Chomsky, on the other hand, believes that we can learn a language because we are born with a universal grammar – a basic understanding of how communication is structured. Linguists such as Chomsky have advocated for a universal grammar since children all around the world develop language in very similar ways over short periods of time with minimal help. The language features inherent in the human mind make up 'Universal Grammar,' which consists of a collection of fundamental principles that apply to all grammars and leave certain parameters open; Universal Grammar determines the bounds within which human languages can vary, rather than specific rules or grammars. Noam Chomsky's political works, with their trademark focus, intensity, and optimism, represent a set of more fundamental convictions about human nature, justice, and social order that are not simply questions of truth. Chomsky's own view of human nature combines a romantic emphasis on the unique human capacity for creative expression with a rationalist claim that the human mind has an intrinsic and determinate structure. The "fundamental fact about the regular use of language," according to Chomsky, is its "creative aspect." Virtually all human beings acquire the linguistic information expressed in such creativity in a short amount of time, and in the face of unstructured and poor environmental inputs. Chomsky, on the other hand, demonstrated clearly that language is far too complicated to be learnt using Skinner's behaviourist approach. Chomsky's review heralded the end of behaviourist learning theories' widespread adoption.

VIEWS OF WHORF ON LANGUAGE DEVELOPMENT

Source: www.ling.yale.edu

Benjamin Whorf (1897–1941), a pioneering linguist, understood the relationship between human language and human thinking: how language may change our innermost thoughts. His central theory is that the structure of the languages we use has a significant impact on our perceptions of the world and our ways of thinking about it. Under investigation, his case for a significant linguistic relativity vanishes. The only way that language clearly and definitely influences mind is in the way that it provides us with the majority of our conceptions. The subject of language and cognition is rejected as trivial and inconsequential, yet it is also asserted (almost casually) that language provides us with the majority of our concepts—a viewpoint significantly stronger than that of even the most pro-Whorf academics. Whorf was not the first to suggest that language had an impact on one's thinking. For example, Humboldt (1836) considered language to be the formative organ of mind, believing that idea and language are inextricably linked (see Gumperz and Levinson 1996a; Lucy 1996, for reviews). Whorf's own opinions were more nuanced than most people think. Whorf proposed that there was a pre-linguistic stratum that organised linguistic and cultural experience, "a universal... way of linking experiences that shows up in laboratory experiments and appears to be independent of language-basically alike for all persons," according to Whorf. A completely different reason for choosing a developmental approach is that it can provide vital indications concerning the system's eventual complexities. Whorf is the most well-known name in linguistics and philosophy, and is associated with the idea that language shapes our perceptions of reality. After a critical examination of Whorf's linguistic relativity principle, I conclude that it is not language as a system that connects language thought and world view, but rather the use of language according to the rules of language games, especially if a particular usage becomes the widely accepted norm. This customary norm finds its way into argumentative discourse in the form of background assumptions included in arguments' premises. Traditional points of view and popular ideologies in a culture can thus be maintained and stabilised in linguistics and philosophy connected with the premise that language plays a decisive role in creating our perception of reality, even if they are questioned in conversations. After a critical examination of Whorf's linguistic relativity principle, I conclude that it is not language as a system that connects language thought and world view, but rather the use of language according to the rules of language games, especially if a particular usage becomes the widely accepted norm. This customary norm finds its way into argumentative discourse in the form of background assumptions included in arguments' premises. Traditional points of view and dominant ideas in a society can thus be perpetuated and consolidated, even when they are questioned in debates.

While researching Indian tribes in the southwestern United States in the 1930s and early 1940s, Benjamin Lee Whorf was intrigued by the disparities in linguistic structure and mental attitude between them and West European languages. He was long fascinated by the diversity of languages as well as their specificity, and he delved into the mysteries of their differences. He became aware of the deeper structures of language via careful study and observation, and he discovered particular mental outlooks that corresponded to each language. As a result, he came up with the concepts of linguistic relativity and Svorld perspective. Whorf's achievement is a bold, though hesitant, move forward in a long-overlooked direction: the ethnic basis of differentiation. Surprisingly, he had stopped short of the logical conclusion. Language had previously appeared to be a natural beginning point—but not any longer.

CONCLUSION

Given the ideological and intellectual context of the period, his conclusions could have been questioned; it could have been said that he was leaning too far in the direction of ethnicity—an approach that could have been interpreted as reactionary nationalism! The gap in Whorf's reasoning is obvious when seen objectively, because every language is the particular speaking behaviour of a speech group. Whorf's worldview was essentially the perspective of an ethnic group. As a man of his time, it is unlikely that he realised that ethnological and linguistic observations must be linked to ethnic issues. He only needed to take one more step forward to recognise an ethnically evolved human society in the very distinct speech community and its language—and the foundation of the vast range of languages and their respective speech communities that had piqued his interest.

REFERENCES

Tohidian, I. (2009). Examining linguistic relativity hypothesis as one of the main views on the relationship between language and thought. Journal of Psycholinguistic Research, 38(1), 65-74.

Byrnes, J. P., & Gelman, S. A. (1991). Perspectives on thought and language: Traditional and contemporary views. Gelman and Byrnes, 1991, 3-27.

Jessel, L. (1978). Whorf: The differentiation of language.

Whorf, B. L. (2012). Language, thought, and reality: Selected writings of Benjamin Lee Whorf. MIT press.

Freeman, D. E., & Freeman, Y. S. (2004). Essential linguistics. What You Need to.

Smith, N., & Allott, N. (2016). Chomsky: Ideas and ideals. Cambridge University Press.

Cook, V. J. (1985). Chomsky's universal grammar and second language learning. Applied linguistics, 6(1), 2-18.

Barman, B. (2012). The linguistic philosophy of Noam Chomsky. Philosophy and Progress, 103-122.

Reed, E. S. (1995). The ecological approach to language development: a radical solution to Chomsky's and Quine's problems. Language & Communication, 15(1), 1-29.

XII
INTELLIGENCE AND CREATIVITY

PRANATI DAS, Student, BBA, Meerabai Institute of Technology
INTRODUCTION
Intelligence and Creativity
Intelligence is a broad concept that encompasses many different aspects of cognition. There has been a slew of theories proposed to explain what intelligence is and how it works. Sternberg's triarchic theory of intelligence emphasizes analytical, creative, and practical intelligence, while Gardner's theory claims that intelligence is made up of many variables. Other theories place a strong emphasis on emotional intelligence. A four-and-a-half-year-old child sits at the kitchen table with his father, who is reading him a new story. He begins to turn the page to resume reading, but the child cries, "Wait, Daddy!" before he can do so. "Pig, go! He exclaims, "Go!" as he points to the text on the new page. The father comes to a complete stop and faces his son. "Can you read that?" he asks. The child exclaims, "Yes, Daddy!" "Pig, go! "Go!" he exclaims once more, pointing to the words. This father was not actively teaching his kid to read, despite the boy's numerous questions about letters, words, and symbols that they encountered everywhere: in the car, in the store, on television. The father wanted to see what else his son could understand, so he decided to do an experiment. He scribbled a list of simple words on a sheet of blank paper: mom, dad, dog, bird, bed, truck, car, tree. He put the list in front of the child and asked him to read the words. He read carefully enough to pronounce the words bird and truck correctly.

"Mom, dad, dog, bird, bed, truck, car, tree," he said. She inquires, "Did I do it, Daddy?" "Of course, you did! That's incredible." The father gave his son a warm hug and continued reading the pig story, all the while wondering if his son's abilities reflected extraordinary genius or just a normal pattern of linguistic development. Psychologists have wondered what intelligence is and how it might be assessed, much like the father in this story.

Classification of Intelligence

What precisely is intelligence? Researchers have revised their definitions of intelligence countless times since the beginning of psychology. A British psychologist named Charles Spearman believed that intelligence was made up of a single general component called g that could be measured and compared between people. Spearman emphasized the commonalities while downplaying the differences among various intellectual talents. Great thinkers like Aristotle, who lived long before modern psychology, held a similar attitude. Others believe that intelligence is more of a combination of skills than a single factor. In the 1940s, Raymond Cattell proposed a theory of intelligence that divided general intelligence into two categories: **crystallized intelligence** and **fluid intelligence**. Crystallized intellect possesses acquired information as well as the ability to regain it. When you learn, remember, and recall information, you use **crystallized intelligence**. In your education, you constantly display crystallized intelligence by demonstrating that you have mastered the content. Fluid intelligence is defined as the ability to recognize complicated relationships and solve problems. After being detoured into an unknown route owing to road construction, your fluid mind would be required to navigate your way home. **Fluid intelligence** helps you overcome intricate, abstract challenges in your daily life, whereas crystallized intelligence helps you overcome real, straightforward issues.

Practical intelligence: -

Sternberg's concept of practical intelligence is commonly referred to as "street smarts." Being practical involves utilizing knowledge based on your experiences to discover solutions that work in your daily life. This sort of intelligence appears to be distinct from traditional IQ; people with high practical intelligence scores may or may not have comparable creative and analytical intelligence scores.

The shootings at Virginia Tech demonstrate both high and low practical intelligences. During the incident, one girl left her class to go buy a Coke at an adjacent building. She wanted to return to class, but when she returned to her building after purchasing her drink, she noticed that the exit door had been locked from the inside. Instead of pondering about why there was a chain around the door knobs, she went to her class's window and snuck back inside. She may have thereby exposed herself to the gunman. Thankfully, she was not shot. On the other hand, a few of students were roaming around campus when they heard gunshots nearby. One friend said, "Let's go check it out and see what's going on." "No way," the other student said, "we have to get away from the gunshots." They did exactly what they said they were going to do. As a result, neither of them sustained any injuries. Although the student who crawled through the window shown considerable ingenuity, he lacked common sense. She'd have a low practical intelligence level. The student who persuaded his friend to run away from gunshots would have much greater practical intelligence.

Analytical intelligence: -

Analytical intelligence is inextricably tied to academic problem solving and computations. According to Sternberg, analytical intelligence is demonstrated by the ability to analyses, appraise, judge, compare, and contrast. It's customary to investigate the motives of the book's main characters or research the story's historical background when reading a classic novel for literature class, for example. In a science course such as anatomy, you must learn how the body uses various minerals in various human systems. To obtain a deeper understanding of this subject, you're use analytical intelligence. When confronted with a tough math problem, you would employ analytical intelligence to investigate numerous aspects of the problem before tackling it section by section.

Creative intelligence: -

An indication of creative intelligence is coming up with or inventing a solution to a problem or scenario. In this discipline, finding a creative solution to an unexpected problem, creating a beautiful work of art, or writing a well-developed short story are all instances of creativity. Consider yourself camping in the woods with some friends when you realize you've left your camp coffee pot at home. The employee who succeeds in preparing coffee for everyone in your company is regarded as having excellent creative intelligence.

Multiple intelligences theory: -

The Multiple Intelligences Theory was developed by Howard Gardner, a Harvard psychologist and Erik Erikson's former student. Gardner's idea, which has been improved for more than 30 years, is a more recent advance among intelligence hypotheses. Gardner believes that each person possesses at least eight intelligences. In most cases, a person excels in some of these eight intelligences while failing in others.

Gardner's concept is still in the works, and additional research is needed to demonstrate its empirical validity. Despite suggestions that Gardner just renamed what other theorists labelled "intelligence," his theories broaden the common definition of intelligence to embrace a larger variety of abilities "Intelligences" as "cognitive styles" (Morgan, 1996). Furthermore, traditional Gardner intelligence tests are extremely difficult to develop. Emotional intelligence is a term used to describe Gardner's interpersonal and intrapersonal intelligences.

Emotional Intelligence: -

Emotional intelligence is defined as the ability to detect and understand one's own and others' emotions, to display empathy, to interpret social interactions and cues, to manage one's own emotions, and to act in a culturally appropriate manner. Those with high emotional intelligence usually have well-developed social skills. According to Daniel Goleman, author of Emotional Intelligence: Why It Can Matter More Than IQ, emotional intelligence is a better predictor of success than standard intelligence. Emotional intelligence, on the other hand, has sparked a lot of debate, with experts pointing out inconsistencies in how it is defined and depicted, as well as casting doubt on the findings of research on a tough subject to quantify and analyses experimentally.

Intelligence can have diverse meanings and values in different cultures. Knowing how to fish and repair a boat is crucial if you live on a small island where the majority of people get their food through fishing from boats. If you were a fantastic fisherman, your coworkers would most certainly perceive you as intelligent. Your brilliance would undoubtedly be known around the island if you could also mend boats. Consider the customs of your own family.

In some cultures, working together as a group is highly appreciated. In these civilizations, the importance of group achievement outweighs the importance of individual achievement. When you visit a culture, your cultural intelligence, also known as cultural competency, is determined by how well you relate to its ideals.

Creativity

Someone is said to be creative if they come up with an innovative idea. An example is a creative solution to a difficult problem. But how can you tell if a notion or solution is innovative? Creativity is defined as the ability to conceive, invent, or discover new ideas, solutions, or possibilities. People who are extremely creative frequently have a strong understanding of a subject, work on it for years, contemplate new solutions, seek out the advice and support of other experts, and take risks. Despite the fact that creativity is often associated with the arts, it is a critical type of intelligence that drives people from all areas of life to try new things. Creativity may be found in every facet of life; from the way you decorate your home to a novel way of understanding how a cell works.

Although several definitions of creativity have been given by psychologists, the one most recently derived from the three criteria used by the United States Patent Office to decide whether an invention is patentable is likely the best.

The first criteria are originality. The concept must have a slim likelihood of becoming a reality. In reality, it should be distinguished on a frequent basis. Albert Einstein's special theory of relativity clearly fulfils this condition. There was no other scientist who thought of the idea.

What is Creative Process?

The flow of thoughts and actions that leads to the final shape of an idea is referred to as the creative process. The creative process necessitates critical thinking and problem-solving talents. From musicians to television producers, the five phases that creative people go through to bring their ideas to life are preparation, incubation, illumination, evaluation, and verification. The stages were first articulated by Graham Wallas, a social psychologist and co-founder of the London School of Economics, in his book The Art of Thought, which outlined the essential stages of the creative process.

The 5 stages of the Creative Process

While each artist approaches their work in their own unique way, most artists move through five stages subconsciously while working on their projects. Each of the five stages of the creative process leads to the next in a logical sequence. As you begin your own creative process, relax your mind and allow your ideas to develop through the five stages of creativity.

· **Preparation stage: -**

The initial step of the creative process entails preparation and idea development. This is when you gather information and perform study in order to come up with a novel idea. To develop divergent thinking, brainstorm and allow your thoughts wander, or write in a notebook; this will help you consider all conceivable routes to fleshing out your concept. The first stage of the process involves your brain accessing its memory bank to produce new ideas by drawing on previous information and experiences.

- **Incubation stage: -**

The second stage is to let go of your concept once you've finished actively thinking about it. Taking a step back from your concept before fleshing it out is an important part of creative thinking. You may focus on another project or take a break from the creative process entirely—whatever the case may be, you are not actively working on your idea. While it may appear counterproductive to walk away from your concept, it is a vital step in the process. Your narrative, song, or problem is incubating in the back of your mind during this period.

- **Illumination stage: -**

The lighting stage, often known as the "aha" moment, occurs when the "aha" moment occurs. As new connections emerge spontaneously, the light bulb goes out, and all of the information you've acquired comes together to present the solution to your problem. The answer to your creative quest comes to you in this third step. For example, you can get over writer's block by deciding out your story's ending. It may catch you off guard, but an idea has developed after the incubation period.

- **Evaluation stage: -**

During this stage, you evaluate the feasibility of your proposal and compare it to alternatives. This is also a moment for introspection, as you review your original notion or problem to evaluate if your solution matches your original vision. Market research may be conducted by business professionals to determine the viability of the concept. During this stage, you can either go back to the drawing board or keep going, confident in what you've created.

- **Verification stage: -**

This is when the creative process comes to a close. It's at this point when the real job begins. A physical object, an advertising campaign, a song, a novel, an architectural design—any item or object that you set out to produce, propelled by that initial thought that jumped into your head—could be your creative product. Now it's time to finish your design, bring your concept to life, and share it with the rest of the world.

Role of school in foresting creativity

A good classroom setting always includes some creative features, which make learning more engaging and participatory. The perfect combination of creativity and education allows pupils to be imaginative and learn new things. Students can improve their emotional and social abilities while also becoming better communicators. Creative classrooms have the potential to change the way students learn and apply what they learn in the real world. In truth, a student's emotional growth is aided by artistic expression. Let's take a look at how vital creativity is in today's classroom and the benefits it provides.

· **Learn with fun: -**

Students can learn while having a good time in a creative classroom. Teaching methods like storytelling and skits allow students to learn without feeling rushed.

Students are usually up for a good time, and incorporating creative activities into the curriculum increases their enthusiasm for learning.

Teachers should develop this quality in pupils as early as the primary grades, inspiring them to believe in their own inventiveness.

Fun team building exercises can be designed to encourage creative thinking in groups and to teach people how to accept the ideas of others.

· **Freedom of expression: -**

In contrast to traditional teaching approaches, creative classrooms allow them to express themselves. Students get the opportunity to come out of their shells and participate in debates, classroom discussions, and field trips. They feel wonderful and happy because of their freedom of expression.

Contributing to the learning sessions provides them a sense of accomplishment as well. A creative learning technique opens them up to the puzzles that come their way and offers them a sense of accomplishment and pride.

• Emotional development: -

A child's emotional development depends on their ability to express themselves creatively. Importantly, this must occur in their lower classes as well, so that they grow up by responding appropriately to events in their environment.

They have the freedom to explore their surroundings and discover new things because of their creativity.

Students will always appreciate a school environment that allows them to explore freely without being restricted. They will gain confidence when they are able to express their actual emotions in a creative manner in their classrooms.

• Enhances thinking capability: -

Students' innovative thinking abilities can be stimulated through creativity. In the middle of demanding curriculum schedules, teachers advocate activities such as open-ended questions, creative team building activities, brainstorming sessions, and discussions.

Some teachers utilize these strategies deftly to teach difficult concepts in a way that students like. Puppet performances, for example, will keep students engaged in the learning sessions, and the flow of images in their minds will provide them with the pleasure of creativity. They will be able to come up with inventive replies to the open-ended questions, which will open up a world of imaginative thinking for them.

• Reduced stress and anxiety: -

It relieves a lot of tension from pupils when some time is made aside for creativity in between all of the tough study sessions. This joy keeps them relaxed and minimizes their anxiety, allowing them to prepare well for exams and perform well on them.

Including more hands-on learning and allowing for visual reflection will have a significant impact. Encouraging fruitful debates and making the classroom arrangement more adaptable are all important factors in creating a creative learning environment.

- **Boost's problem-solving skills: -**

Children's problem-solving skills can be stimulated through brainstorming sessions using puzzles.

Creativity may drastically affect how students approach an issue, and it can leave them feeling incredibly positive after participating in creative teaching sessions.

In order to help kids, think outside the box and be more inventive and original, creative problem solving can be encouraged in the classroom.

Students will reinterpret the issues or possibilities in this manner, and the answers or replies will be more imaginative.

- **Improves focus and attention: -**

A lower-class child's average attention or concentration span is only a few minutes. Traditional instructional methods would bore them, and they might lose interest in the middle.

Incorporating creative teaching tactics such as storytelling and skits will undoubtedly boost their focus and attention, resulting in more effective study time.

Playing memory games, taking regular breaks and intervals to encourage creativity, and creating a flexible classroom environment will help them enhance their attention span significantly.

- **Better communication: -**

They can improve their attention span greatly by playing memory games, taking regular breaks and intervals to foster creativity, and providing a flexible classroom environment. Classroom arguments not only help children think creatively, but they also help them comprehend and accept the perspectives of others. This type of collaborative creative experience encourages kids to open up and become better communicators.

- **Follow passion: -**

It is critical for a student to pursue their passions in addition to succeeding in academics if they are to be successful in life. A good classroom setting should allow pupils to pursue their interests in music, dance, poetry, sketching, and other forms of art.

This makes kids feel happy, which allows them to approach academics with an open mind.

Setting aside time for such activities can help kids improve their creative abilities as well as their academic abilities. Students who make the best use of these chances can graduate with honors.

- **Future opportunities: -**

Charts that depict the goals, along with timetables, can help students keep track of their progress in a challenging classroom. Students gain the foundation for how successful they can be when they grow up in the school.

The abilities and confidence students develop throughout their school years will have a significant impact on how they progress in their careers.

In reality, those with a creative skill set have an advantage over those with a purely academic skill set in terms of triggering future chances. During the knockout stages, they are allowed to express themselves, and how they show themselves is extremely important in this competitive period.

- **Innovative mindset: -**

Two common creative teaching tactics that help students develop an innovative mentality are open-ended questions and classroom debates. Students are given the opportunity to think critically about the situation or subject at hand and to come up with novel solutions.

The amicable classroom conversations also help kids think critically about other people's ideas and contributions in order to create something new. Lower-class pupils can benefit from a lively classroom environment that is colorful rather than black and white, and teachers might make an attempt to include some comedy in between sessions.

- **Drive Lifelong Learning: -**

A person with a creative mindset has a constant desire to learn new things, which allows them to enjoy the wonderful sense of lifelong learning.

This would keep them interested and busy throughout the day, allowing them to stay young at all times. An inquisitive mind is constantly eager to learn more, and creative classrooms can help children develop a curious attitude in unique ways.

With the rising mobile industry, education apps are on the rise, and there are several fantastic apps that encourage creativity, such as Doodle Buddy, 123D Sculpt, Audacity, and GarageBand.

It is, however, the responsibility of a good teacher to bring the correct mix of creativity into the classroom and to bring out the best in students.

The pleasure of creativity also contributes significantly to improved health, allowing them to continue to flourish academically and in the field of creative.

CONCLUSION

The ability to acquire and apply knowledge is how intelligence is traditionally characterized. In testing situations, one's capacity to use historical information is used to determine one's Intelligence Quotient (IQ).

The ability to come up with new ideas through a mental process of connecting existing notions is referred to as creativity. The ideas don't have to be revolutionary (a common misperception about creative thinking), but they do have to be novel to the thinker.

Intelligence does have a role in creative thinking, but not in the way you may imagine.

In general, your IQ is determined by your capacity to interpret data and give solutions, regardless of the situation. IQ is extremely significant in mathematics and basic sciences since it displays your capacity to recall concepts and apply them to similar issues. If I tell you that two plus two equals four, you should be able to deduce that four plus four equals double the original answer (ideally).

This fact alone indicates intelligence's link to creativity, which is critical for not just understanding but also increasing creative thinking. Another crucial feature of intelligence is the ability to effectively filter solutions.

To summaries, expert creatives do not have to be smarter than the typical person. They simply do three things better than anyone else: they have more experiences, they reflect on their experiences more frequently, and when pursuing potential solutions to problems or projects, they simply work harder with the ideas they generate (whereas everyone else gives up after evaluating just one or two possible ideas, or by letting their inner critic prevent them from exploring more).

REFERENCES: -

- https://courses.lumenlearning.com/.../what-are-intelligence-and-creativity
- https://ideapod.com/the-creative-process/
- https://www.oecd.org/education/fostering-students-creativity-and
- https://creativesomething.net/post/41103661291/the-relationship

XIII

PSYCHOLOGY OF LEARNERS AND BETTERMENT OF LEARNER'S ATTITUDES IN LEARNING PROCESS

Dr. Hafiz Nasir Ali , Lecturer (Visiting), University of Sargodha, Sub Campus Bhakkar, District Bhakkar

Dr. Tariq Mahmood ,Research Scholar, Department of Islamic Studies, B.Z.U. Multan, Pakistan

Ms. Sidrah Urooj Niazi,Master in English, Officer Grade in Danish High School for girls, Distt. Mianwali

Abstract

This paper presents discussion about the different level of learners and the psychology of learners in the learning place. The purpose of this paper is to highlight the learner's role in the learning activities, whether these activities are done in the home or outside the home, i.e. in schools or in other learning places. The paper presents that learning activities will be useful if learners, trainers and management of training are providing its role in best way and in honestly. In this paper, it is discussed that wrong actions of learners requires special guidance which can be modified in good

"

attitude of learners by the trainers if they understand the economic and social problems of learners in learning process. Similarly, teachers will have to keep in mind the age of learners and mental approach of learners so that problem behind attitudes, their weaknesses can be changed. Anyhow, in this paper, role of religious education is also highlighted to elaborate the good values and promotion of level of soul.

Key Words: Learners; Teachers; Psychology; Children; Adolescent; Attitudes.

INTRODUCTION

It is fact that psychology deals with attitude and characters of learners in learning process. In learning process, it is mandatory for the teacher to know about the learners' personality and his family background for fruitful results from learners in learning process.

The learning of environment plays a significant role in brain development. As, adolescent performs an important mental task. The neural network that supports those abilities strengthen necessary their cognitive, emotion-regulate a memory skills. Without opportunities to use these skills, these networks remain under-developed making it challenging for individuals to engage in higher order thinker as adults. [i] (Robyn Harper, August 2018)

In the materialistic world of mundane life, generally, prefer solution of body requirements rather than development of soul requirements. Every religion and its teachings help us to promote religious and spiritual values that make us civilized and helpful for humanity. Therefore, in learning process, both worldly and spiritual must be fulfilled for the betterment of learners. Otherwise, without spiritual and civilized education, degree may be attained in worldly institutions but the person may be manners-less after neglecting the manners and spiritual teachings of any religion of the world.

There are different types of psychologies but social psychology is that psychology which studies the behavior of mankind. But the requirements of body and soul are different while every man is compound of soul and body. The soul is invisible while body is visible. In societies, there are active and popular organizations on the basis characters of their members or employees or combination of management and members also.[ii] (Masood Tahira Dr., 2017)

Anyhow, behind any person's behavior, there are many factors that influence particular person to adopt strict or soft corner in behavior. In this, past incidents of his life, past accidents of relatives or friends and his current financial position and current friend or relatives attitudes to this particular are also.

As author of 'Social Psychology', stated that behind person's attitudes, past events effect his behavior regarding present thing.[iii] (Mughal Tariq Mahmood, 2013) In the present world, fact is that if any person is deceived by some other person of any other particular tribe or of particular department, definitely, his behavior will be bitter in future on the bases of past events about persons of this particular tribe or department. Similarly, if any learner gets good guidance and feels impressive from any institution, definitely in future, that particular person will have positive views and guides other to get admission in this institution as proposal.

Similarly, in the changing of persons' behaviors, current incidents or losses make persons bitter regarding behavior of the people of societies. [iv] (Mughal Tariq Mahmood, 2013) In societies, if you want spread positive activities then it is necessary that positive values must be encouraged and the persons who are uncivilized, these must be discouraged and their weaknesses must be pinpointed for correction not for discussion.

In educational institutions, generally, teachers' attitude about hard working students and intelligent students remain positive and mostly teachers appreciate these types of learners due to their efficacy in studies. Similarly in any organization, hardworking and efficient worker will be encouraged in the eyes of his boss. Therefore, in educational institutions such types of steps must be taken so that teacher could involve students in teaching activities. In this way, students can become hard working and civilized if regular care is done.

In learning process in schools, the teacher's behavior about the students who complete their work, will be good and favorable rather than those who do not do homework or dull in class activities. [v] (Bhutta Waqar Ahmad, 2009) It is the duty of teachers that they should not neglect the dull students in learning activities so that they can improve their educational weaknesses. It is my practical experience that with proper care, dull and weak students are improved with the passage of time. While if these are neglected and not provided proper care, they leave their studies in early age.

Furthermore, if someone wants to change person's behaviors then by creating difficult situation about future or danger of foreign attack, changing in behavior of the people may occur.[vi] (Mansoor Ali Akbar, 1998) As in the perceptions of war, or danger of war, mostly people will increase shopping than demand due to danger of war. Similarly if educated persons are employed on heavy earnings, this will be encouragement for the present learners to study more on the hope of good paying jobs. If educated persons remain un-employed or can gain low level of income. This will be actually discouragement for present learners so that they will continue study without any interest.

Anyhow, some scholars opine that teachers can correct the behaviors of their students' attitude if they are not doing well. While some others opine that teachers cannot correct students' attitude because they favor of the given quotation, 'Nature cannot change.' Anyhow, changing of students' attitude may be improved in some students while in some students, teachers' guidance may not be improved but for very low number, this may be occurred.

Teachers cannot actually control their students' behavior. That's because the only behavior, person can control in his or her own. And when teachers try directly to restrict what say or do, they are usually left feelings frustrated and helpless. [vii] (Shari Gent, March 22, 2021)

Training of individual is crucial for the promotion of civilized society. In actual, training of individuals in present time will show its results/outcomes in future. This is why, in every department of any country, training is provided for its employees so that particular sense might be developed.

As, Allama Asad wrote that, societies can built only in the result of trainings and polite behaviors of trainers which are used in learning manners. [viii] (Muhammad Asad Allama, March 2009) learners' attitude may be affected from the attitude of teachers or master trainers in learning or training activities. Similarly, if teachers' behavior is impressive then learners will be attracted from his style.

Similarly if teacher will use rude behavior in teaching or in learning activities, this will be dangerous for students and students will feel boredom. Therefore, learning process must be as so that learners feel happy in learning process.

And teachers can control the wrong activities of students in class by presenting such style and manner so that concerning involved student try to avoid from wrong behavior or unsuitable behavior.[ix] (Shari Gent, March 22, 2021) Besides these, if wrong behavior is not corrected by the teacher, or if teachers continue teaching activities and students remain busy in their wrong activities in class, This means both groups are just spending their time, or it may be stated that time is being killed. Therefore, it is better for fruitful results in learning for the students and for the teachers that both should take interest fully. And teachers should perform their duties having fear of God with honestly. Same is upon for learners otherwise there is need to change students attitude regarding learning.

While Edward Kang stated that, teacher can guide students to avoid ineffective studying habits in favor of ones that will increase their learning outcomes. Too often people imagine that long hours of studying are the best path to being a model straight a student. Yet research shows that highly successful students actually spend less time studying than their peers' do-they just study more effectively. [x] (Edward Kang, April 4, 2019)

As concerned the responsibility of teachers or learners concerned, this may be stated that children are innocent so they influence from things and people at once. Therefore, teachers and parents are more responsible as they know the time, the people, about good or bad values and attitudes of the people with their effects. This may supported from Meaning of Holy Prophet's sayings that every child takes his birth in nature but it is upon his parents that make him, Muslim, Jew, Christian or follower of any other religion. The reason is that children are innocents so elders, the old and others are responsible to keep the children on track of success.

And Emma Chippa stated that students are just like agriculture and plants, as you will care the plants safe from any kinds of raw roots or grass, then they will be grow safely otherwise, there will be problem to grow safely and to become civilized[xi]. (Emma Chiappetta, June 18, 2021)

It is empirical evidence that sometimes, educated parents cannot provide better guidance and better learning institution but sometimes uneducated persons can provide better guidance and learning environment. Due to this, the children / learners of uneducated persons can achieve good marks and good values in the societies. This also refers that theoretical values are different from practical values. And for attaining good and civilized values/ manners, adoption of practical values will be useful.

While Edward Kang stated that there are following recommended techniques for high intensity study habits. These are as under:

I.   Pre-test;
II. Spaced practice;
III. Self-Quizzing;
IV. Inter-learning practice;
V.   Paraphrasing & Reflecting.[xii] (Edward Kang, April 4, 2019)

For fruitful learning and better techniques, the learner must involve himself in studying activities. And for preparation of any test, learner must analyze himself by self-test before taking any test so that he can remove mistakes and shortcoming before the actual test time. The advantage of pre-test activities will be useful as it will provide chance to paraphrase the sentences.

In Amin's views, habits become nature when actions are repeated again and again.[xiii] (Muhammad Amin Dr., 2004). In classes, it is duty of teachers and in homes; it is duty of parents that they must know about actions of their young ones so that proper solution for these actions must be proposed.

Without considering this, this habit is useful or not useful, or this habit is good for individuals or for societies. In learning institutions, it is the duty of teacher and management of institutions to provide better conditions for learning activities so that learner can adopt positive and cultured values.

The fact is that sociologists opine that the purpose of social and welfare organizations is to provide satisfaction to humanity regarding their needs. Therefore, mostly organizations are established especially for the promotion of availability of basic needs without considering, caste, creed and color. [xiv] (Bhutta Waqar Ahmad, 2009)

In a comprehensive report about madaris, it is presented that these are spreading mostly positive values besides these, some are promoting particular school of thought which is against unity of Muslim. [xv] (Editor/compiler, 1988) In an analysis about religious madaris of different countries, it is known that religious madaris are more fruitful regarding religious education or for preparation of hereafter life rather than worldly or mundane life of Muslims. But formal and non-formal institutions are preparing just for mundane life rather than hereafter life. Therefore, it may be stated that present scenario, for Muslims, from educational institutions, madaris are more useful than formal schools or colleges or universities only for religious activities and religious education. But the drawback of madaris is that, in this separate school of thought is stressed rather than remain united even within the Muslims. Similarly, in Hindus, or Christians, separate education is provided regarding their religions.

Here, it may be stated that worldly education and the religious education has been divided in different categories among all religion in present era. This is why, educated of one particular school of thought has different point of view about the educated and qualified person of other school of thought or religion. This is the main base of discrimination among the scholars of different institutions in different countries of the world.

It is reality that if you want to know about the level of civilization of any society, or any nation, then from the level of crimes, it may be analyzed that this society or nation is civilized or not. If crimes ratio is low, it refers that people are civilized and these are busy in learning and positive activities.

In Rehman's views those societies promote and become popular in which negative actions and values are discouraged while good values are encouraged by the individuals and by the societies without considering its results. [xvi] (Rehman Khalid, 2010)

It may be stated from Rehman's views that good qualities and values notify about the level and standard of society. In any society, crimes are increasing and culprits are not sentenced. This refers that in this society, wrong activities are not discouraged or justice system is not working properly. The reason of increasing crime is also easiness and shirking behavior from hardworking. Therefore, such steps must be taken for learners in the institutions so that they could do their work in taking interest and with hard working. Hard working ability will be useful in all the sectors of life in future.

In Saleem's views success is in the hardworking. Those nations become the habitual of hardworking, one day or next day, they can become to see their success. [xvii] (Khalid saleem Mansoor, 2003) From Saleems' views, it may be stated that from learners' activities, it may be stated that learner will become successful nation in future or not, If the learners of any nation are hard working in their activities, this refers to identify that these learners will soon attain their goal whatever they have set it in their minds. The reason is that it is famous quotation that hardworking is the key to success.

History also shows that great scholars and scientists and great leaders of the world all have common quality/ability i.e. hardworking. With the help of hardworking ability or habit, learners can achieve their goals as intelligent can achieve.

In Shahab's views, as concerned the difference of learning is just like the difference of Muslims' actions.[xviii] (Shahab Qudratullah, 2004) As concerned Shahab's views, he want say that learning process in different institutions is different because of practical role of teachers/ Muslims. Here, it may be stated that learners are influence from the person they are being provided learning activities. Therefore if a teacher is practical Muslim or practical Hindus or of other religion, then learners will be more attractive from his activities than that person who is not good in his character whether he is a Muslim or Non-Muslim. It may be derived that teacher's role has also influence to the learners. Besides teachers' role, schools/ institutions and management role are not neglect able.

In Monique's point of view, schools can play an important role in adolescents' identity development. No doubt, all adolescents are not same. There are three types of groups of adolescents regarding their abilities.[xix] (Monique Verhoeven, Astrid Mita poortuis & Monique Volman, March, 2019) It is fact that the role of schools, colleges or universities may be impressive for learners if its management provide complete facilities to the learners and learning activities are done without wasting time. In this type of institutions, students' knowledge will increase and student will feel satisfaction in the core of their hearts. And these students will become the advertiser of this particular school/college/ university/ institution. Otherwise, student will not consider good about this institution.

CONCLUSION

In nutshell, it may be stated that learning activities must be impressive for the learners so that it may guide dull and weak learners separately with special care. In learning activities, teachers' role or role of master trainer cannot be ignored. Furthermore, learners' role and their attitude may be changed if some are not taking interest in learning activities. Teachers and the mater trainers also keep in mind that their attitude also must be for the betterment of learners rather than not just for spending time. No doubt, learners' and trainers' attitude regarding values and manners must be ideal otherwise All these activities and trainer's words will not be fruitful for leaners if he is offering words only from mouth rather than core of hearts. Anyhow, with worldly education, religious education must be provided to the learners of particular religion that will create emotions to help humanity. Any teachers/ trainers must keep in mind, the sociological status and economic condition of learners so that they could behave them in light of condition which will be useful in learning process.

References

[i] Robyn Harper (August 2018), "Science of adolescent affect students learning : How body & brain development affect student learning," retrieved from www.allyed.org, Washington: Alliance for excellent Education, p-1,

[ii] Masood Tahira Dr., (2017) "Why advice is ineffective", Lahore: Monthly periodical Turjuman-ul-quran, p-90.

[iii] Mughal Tariq Mahmood, (2013) " Social Psychology', Lahore: Urdu Science Board, p-206.

[iv] Mughal Tariq Mahmood,(2013) " Social Psychology', Lahore: Urdu Science Board, pp-218-221.

[v] Bhutta Waqar Ahmad," (2009). "Social Work", Lahore: Advanced Publishers, pp-66-67.

[vi] Mansoor Ali Akbar (1998) "Muslim Psychology", Lahore: Feroze Sons,pp-100-1-1.

[vii] Shari Gent, (March 22, 2021) "12 strategies to inspire listening learning and self-control", derived from www. additudemag.com, derived on 16[Th] July, 2021,p-1.

[viii] Muhammad Asad Allama, (March 2009) " importance of Sunnah", Lahore: Turjuman-ul-Quran, pp-33-34.

[ix] Shari Gent, (March 22, 2021) "12 strategies to inspire listening, learning and self-control", derived from www. additudemag.com, derived on 16[Th] July, 2021,pp-2-16.

[x] Edward Kang (April 4, 2019)" Research backed studying techniques, derived from www.edutopia.org, derived on 15th July, 2021, p-1.

[xi] Emma Chiappetta (June 18, 2021) "Cultivating Number sense among middle &high school students", derived from www.edutopia.org, pp-1-5.

[xii] Edward Kang (April 4, 2019)" Research backed studying techniques, derived from www.edutopia.org, derived on 15th July, 2021, pp-1-5.

[xiii] Muhammad Amin Dr., (2004) "Islam aor Tazkiya Nafs", Lahore: Urdu Science Board, pp-607-608.

[xiv] Bhutta Waqar Ahmad," (2009). "Social Work", Lahore: Advanced Publishers, pp-64-66.

[xv] Editor, (1988) " A comprehensive report on Madaris' efficacy" Islamabad: Ministry of religious affairs, pp-8-9.

[xvi] Rehman Khalid (2010) " Deeni Madaris, conditions, prospects and problems", Islamabad: Institute of policy studies, pp-17-19.

[xvii] Khalid saleem Mansoor (2003) "Deeni Madaris mey taleem", Islamabad: Institute of policy studies, pp-30-37.

[xviii] Shahab Qudratullah (2004) "Shahab Nama", Lahore: Sang-e- Meel Publications, pp-230- 240.

[xix] Monique Verhoeven, Astrid Mita poortuis & Monique Volman (March, 2019), " The role of schools in adolescents identity development, A literature Review, Educational Psychology Review Journal, Vol. 31, issue1, pp-1-2.

XIV

LEARNING THEORIES OF PERSONALITY: IVAN PAVLOV

Muskan Jindal ,BA(hons) Psychology, MA Psychology

INTRODUCTION

Learning theory of personality deals with the relationships between stimuli and responses. It falls under the behaviorism where observed behavior presents the model of personality. Behavioral psychology, commonly known as behaviorism, is a learning theory based on the concept that all behaviors are learned through conditioning. Personality, according to the behaviourist viewpoint, is nothing more (or less) than a set of learned behaviour patterns. They are unconcerned about the internal causes of behaviour. Personality is learnt by classical and operant conditioning, observational learning, reinforcement, extinction, generalization, and discrimination, much like any other learned behaviour. Strict behaviourists believed that anyone, regardless of genetic background, personality attributes, or interior thoughts, could theoretically be trained to execute any activity (within the limits of their physical capabilities). Only the proper conditioning is required.

The behavioural learning theory, sometimes known as behaviourism, is a popular notion that focuses on how individuals learn. All behaviours are taught through interaction with the environment, according to behaviourism. According to this learning theory, behaviours are acquired from their environment, and intrinsic or inherited characteristics have very little influence on behaviour.

Keywords: Classical Conditioning, Behaviourism, Response, Stimuli

Ivan Petrovich Pavlov (1849-1936) was born in Ryazan, Russia. He received Nobel prize in 1904 on his work on the physiology of digestion. Pavlov was a skilled versatile surgeon who used dogs as experimental animals to create fistulas from various areas of the digestive tract, allowing him to get salivary gland, pancreas, and liver secretions without disrupting nerve and blood flow. Pavlov was a behaviourist who studied animal behaviour. This suggests that his beliefs were based on observable behaviour, as opposed to cognition, which cannot be quantified. Individual personality characteristics, according to Pavlov, are the outcome of learning and diverse contextual experiences. His theory is based on scientific data. Pavlov researched reflexes, or automatic behaviours triggered by a stimulus in the environment. Some reflexes, such as blinking our eyes when a puff of air enters them or sucking a baby's mouth when something is placed in it, are learned. This automatic response can be influenced. This is referred to as conditioning. According to behavioural psychologists there are two types of conditioning: classical and operant conditioning.

Classical conditioning

In order to study the classical conditioning, Pavlov conducted an experiment. He chose his dog for this experiment. Pavlov began by performing a simple operation on his dog, inserting a rubber tube into the salivary gland to quantify the exact amount of saliva secreted during the trial. Following these preliminary steps, a neutral stimulus (e.g., a bell) was provided for a brief period of time, followed by a second stimulus known to induce salivation response and referred to as the unconditioned stimulus (e.g., Meat Powder). Conditioning trials were undertaken in quick succession, with each combination of conditioned stimulus (CS) and unconditioned stimulus (UCS) serving as a conditioning trial. The CS (bell) developed the ability to elicit salivation as a result of repetitive matching. The conditioned response was named as the salivation to the bell (CR) began only after the training (CR). The salivation response to the meat powder, on the other hand, was called unconditioned response since it seemed to happen automatically (UCR).

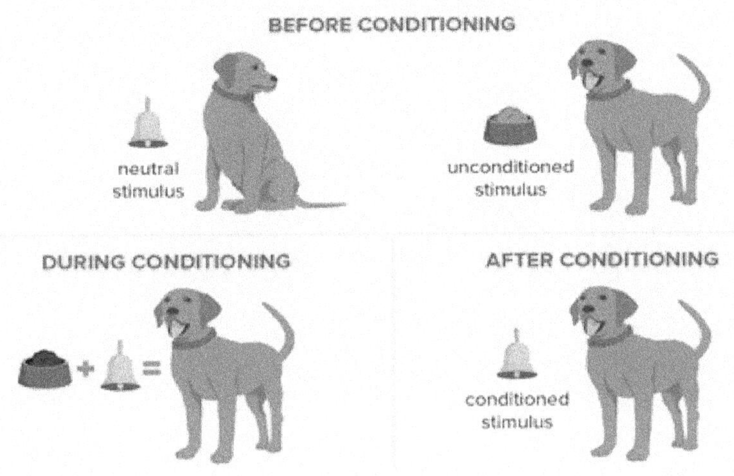

Source: Healthline

To understand the process of classical conditioning, it becomes important to study the stages of conditioning.

There are three phases of conditioning:

Phase1: Before conditioning (Learning)

A naturally occurring stimulus that will automatically elicit a response is required for the initial step of the classical conditioning process. A good example of a naturally occurring stimulus is salivation in reaction to the smell of food. The unconditioned stimulus (UCS) causes an unconditioned response during this stage of the process (UCR). When food is presented (the UCS), for example, a salivation reaction occurs naturally and automatically (the UCR).

Unconditional, natural, and automatic responses are elicited by an unconditioned stimulus. When you smell one of your favorite foods, for example, you may become quite hungry right away. The unconditioned stimulus in this case is the smell of the food. The unconditioned reaction is a natural response to an unconditioned stimulus that occurs without being taught. The unconditioned reaction in our case is a feeling of hunger in response to the smell of food.

Phase 2: During Conditioning

The previously neutral stimulus is repeatedly paired with the unconditioned stimulus during the second phase of the classical conditioning process. The previously neutral stimulus and the unconditioned stimulus create an association as a result of this pair.

Assume if when you smelled your favourite cuisine, you were also greeted by the sound of a whistle. While the whistle has little to do with the smell of the food, if it is repeatedly coupled with the fragrance, the whistle will eventually activate the conditioned reaction. The whistle's tone is the conditioned stimulus in this example.

Phase 3: After conditioning

Once the UCS and the CS have formed a relationship, providing the conditioned stimulus alone will elicit a response even if the unconditioned stimulus is not present. The conditioned response is the resultant response (CR). The learnt response to a previously neutral stimuli is known as the conditioned response. The conditioned response in our scenario would be to feel hungry when you heard the whistle.

Principles of classical conditioning

Classical conditioning has been linked to a number of different occurrences, according to behaviourists. Some of these parts deal with the initial establishment of the response, while others deal with its extinction. Understanding the classical conditioning process requires an understanding of these factors.

1. **Acquisition**

The first stage of learning is acquisition, which is when a reaction is established and subsequently strengthened. A neutral stimulus is repeatedly associated with an unconditioned stimulus during the acquisition phase of classical conditioning.

The number of associations between this stimulus and the unconditioned stimulus is the first factor. As the number of pairings grows, the conditioned stimulus begins to elicit a stronger conditioned response. The size, latency, and likelihood of occurrence of the conditioned response are all used to determine the reaction's intensity. The interval that elapses between the presentation of the conditioned stimulus and the presentation of the unconditioned stimulus is the second factor that has a significant impact on the process of classical conditioning. Conditioning appears to be at its peak for a variety of responses when the interval is 0.50 seconds.

Consider the case of teaching a dog to salivate in response to the sound of a bell. You keep associating the sound of the bell with the appearance of food. When the dog begins to salivate in reaction to the bell tone, you can say the response has been acquired. You can gradually reinforce the salivation response once it has been established to ensure that the behaviour is well learnt.

2. **Extinction**

When the occurrences of a conditioned reaction decrease or cease, it is called extinction. This occurs when a conditioned stimulus is no longer paired with an unconditioned stimulus in classical conditioning. For example, if the smell of food (the unconditioned stimulus) was combined with the sound of a whistle (the conditioned stimulus), the conditioned response of hunger would be elicited. The conditioned response (hunger) would gradually fade if the unconditioned stimulus (the smell of food) was no longer associated with the conditioned stimulus (the whistle).

3. **Spontaneous Recovery**

Even after a period of extinction, a learnt reaction can resurface unexpectedly. The return of the conditioned response after a time of rest or reduced responsiveness is known as spontaneous recovery.

Take this example: after teaching a dog to salivate in reaction to the sound of a bell, you discontinue reinforcing the behaviour, and the response ultimately goes away. You abruptly ring the bell after a rest period during which the conditioned stimulus is not provided, and the animal spontaneously recovers the previously learned reaction.

After a spontaneous recovery, extinction will occur extremely quickly if the conditioned stimulus and unconditioned stimulus are no longer connected.

Applications of classical conditioning

The concepts of classical conditioning have been demonstrated to be extremely effective in changing behaviour. Classical conditioning concepts have also been used in the treatment of neurosis and phobias. Rather than focusing on the basis of the problem like a traditional psychopathologist, a behaviourist could use classical conditioning to eliminate the symptom. The psychopathological sickness of the patient could be cured by supporting the symptom's extinction. (Schwartz & Lacy, 1982).

Classic conditioning has also been demonstrated to be effective in the treatment of alcoholism and nicotine addiction. Addiction develops as a result of both the pleasurable physiological effects of nicotine and alcohol, which are unconditioned stimuli, and the taste of nicotine and alcohol, which are conditioned stimuli, according to Pavlovian principles. It is exceedingly easy to become addicted again when one quits swallowing the chemical, as in standard therapy approaches. After all, "simply not delivering a conditioned stimulus does not remove the relationship between it and unconditioned stimuli" (Schwartz & Lacy, 1982).

References

- Rouleau N, Karbowski LM, Persinger MA. Experimental evidence of classical conditioning and microscopic engrams in an electroconductive material. *PLoS ONE.* 2016;11(10):e0165269. doi:10.1371/journal.pone.0165269
- https://www.healthline.com/health/classical-conditioning
- Holland JG. Behaviorism: Part of the problem or part of the solution. *J Appl Behav Anal.* 1978;11(1):163-74. doi:10.1901/jaba.1978.11-163
- Morè L, Jensen G. Acquisition of conditioned responding in a multiple schedule depends on the reinforcement's temporal contingency with each stimulus. *Learn Mem.* 2014;21(5):258-62. doi: 10.1101/lm.034231.113
- Lattal KM, Lattal KA. Facets of Pavlovian and operant extinction. *Behav Processes.* 2012;90(1):1-8. doi:10.1016/j.beproc.2012.03.009
- Thanellou A, Green JT. Spontaneous recovery but not reinstatement of the extinguished conditioned eyeblink response in the rat. *Behav Neurosci.* 2011;125(4):613-25. doi:10.1037/a0023582
- Boulding, K. E. (1984). B. F. Skinner: A dissident view. *Behavioural and Brain Sciences, 7,* 483-484.
- Gracia, J., McGrown, B. K., & Green, K. F. (1972) Biological constraints on conditioning. In A. H. Black and W. F. Prokasy (Eds) *Classical Conditioning II:Current Research and Theory.* New York: Appleton-Century-Crofts.

- Rescorla, R. A. (1973). Pavlovlian conditioning: It's not what you think it is.*American Psychologist, 43,* 151-160.
- Schwartz, B., & Lacey, H. (1982). *Behaviourism, science, and human nature.*New York: Norton.
- Seligman, M. E. P. (1972). On the generality of the laws of learning. *Psychological eview, 77,* 406-418.

LIST OF AUTHORS

1. **Dr.Anshika Rajvanshi,** Assistant Professor, Department of Management, IIMT, Delhi.
2. **Gurpinder Kumar,** Assistant Professor, Centre for Women's Studies, University of Allahabad, Prayagraj, UP-211002, INDIA.
3. **Dr.Mukta Goyal,** Assistant Professor, Guru Nanak Dev. Institute of Technology, Delhi.Department of management.
4. **Mr. K. C. Malik,** Associate Professor, Sri Venkateswara College, University of Delhi.
5. **Dr. Abhishek Srivastava,** Associate Professor, Faculty of Management Studies, Gopal Narayan Singh University, Rohtas, Bihar.
6. **Dr. Ekata Gupta,**Associate Professor,Guru Nanak Institute of management, Delhi.
7. **Mr.Anand Prakash Dube,**Associate Professor, School of Management Science.
8. **Dr. Hafiz Nasir Ali ,** Lecturer (Visiting), University of Sargodha, Sub Campus Bhakkar, District Bhakkar.
9. **Dr. Tariq Mahmood ,**Research Scholar, Department of Islamic Studies, B.Z.U. Multan, Pakistan.
10. **Ms. Sidrah Urooj Niazi,**Master in English, Officer Grade in Danish High School for girls, Distt. Mianwali.
11. **Tanwangini Sahani,** Student, BBA, GGSIPU, Delhi.
12. **Praniti Das ,** Student, BBA, Meerabai Institute of Technology.
13. **Swati singh,** Student, Guru Nanak Dev. Institute of Technology, Delhi. B.Voc. Software Development.
14. **Kanishka Tomar,** Pupil Teacher, Manvi Institute of Education and Technology, SCERT.
15. **Muskan Jindal,**BA(hons) Psychology, MA Psychology.